A

COLLECTION OF

LESSONS

FROM GRADES 6 THROUGH 8

BY MARILYN BURNS AND CATHY HUMPHREYS

MATH SOLUTIONS PUBLICATIONS

Art Direction and Design: Janet Bollow
Illustration: Martha Weston
Editing: Judith Chaffin
Composition: Alphatype

Printed in the United States of America

ISBN 0-941355-03-9

Distributed by Cuisenaire Company of America, Inc.
P.O. Box 5026
White Plains, New York 10602-5026

Available on Videotape

Some lessons from each book in the series, *A Collection of Math Lessons,* have been
captured on three series of videotapes — *Mathematics with Manipulatives* (K-6),
Mathematics: Teaching for Understanding (K–6), and *Mathematics for Middle School* (6-8).
Classes of elementary and middle school students are taught by Marilyn Burns and other
instructors of Math Solutions.

The videotapes are available from Cuisenaire Company of America, Inc., P.O.Box 5026,
White Plains, NY 10602-5026. For information, telephone (800) 237-3142.

130483

CONTENTS

130483

INTRODUCTION

The National Council of Teachers of Mathematics' *Curriculum and Evaluation Standards for School Mathematics* (1989, 5) presents five general goals for all students:

> (1) that they learn to value mathematics, (2) that they become confident in their ability to do mathematics, (3) that they become mathematical problem solvers, (4) that they learn to communicate mathematically, and (5) that they learn to reason mathematically.

A *Collection of Math Lessons From Grades 6 Through 8* presents examples of ways that these goals can be translated into classroom instruction. The chapters in the book describe actual lessons taught to classes of sixth-, seventh-, and eighth-grade students. Along with presenting the details of the math activities, the lessons model how to organize students into small groups that work cooperatively, how to incorporate the use of concrete materials, and how to integrate writing into math instruction.

There is wide agreement among researchers that a constructive, active view of learning must be reflected in the way mathematics is taught. As stated in *Reshaping School Mathematics* (1990, 3): "Learning is not a process of passively absorbing information and storing it in easily retrievable fragments as a result of repeated practice and reinforcement." Students should have, instead, opportunities to interpret mathematical theories and construct mathematical understandings for themselves. To that end, the lessons in this book engage students actively in problem-solving investigations that have thinking and reasoning as their primary emphasis. In all lessons, the priority is placed on encouraging and valuing students' ideas.

In the title essay of her book, *The Having of Wonderful Ideas* (1987), Eleanor Duckworth makes the case that classroom experiences should aim to capture curiosity, foster resourcefulness, and make knowledge accessible and interesting—with the goal of stimulating students to explore and express their own ideas.

"The having of wonderful ideas is what I consider the essence of intellectual development," Duckworth writes (p. 1). She makes no distinction between ideas that many people have already had and ideas that no one has had before. She writes that the nature of a creative intellectual act is the same in either case. Thus, a child who discovers for him or herself that multiplying a number by 10 results in appending a zero to it has the same quality of experience as does a person who uncovers information that had not yet been discovered.

"The more we help children to have their wonderful ideas," Duckworth concludes, ". . . the more likely it is that they will some day happen upon wonderful ideas that no one else has happened upon before" (p. 14). Duckworth's view describes what math lessons at their best can offer: opportunities for students to interact with important math ideas, make their own connections, and have wonderful ideas of their own.

Because math is traditionally presented to students as a body of information and procedures to be memorized and practiced, by the middle-school years, students' views of mathematics are often deeply solidified in the notion that doing math is merely a matter of applying what they're taught to arrive at correct answers. Understanding takes a back seat and solving new and unexpected problems is the exception. Rarely is learning math for students an activity that has, as its base, the having of wonderful ideas. Some students don't even have a clue about what a wonderful idea in math might look like. A shift is needed so that math lessons give value to the unexpected rather than to learning and repeating the tried and true.

In this book, our lessons have as their goal involving students in doing mathematics. We encourage them to investigate, conjecture, represent, apply, prove, communicate—those practices that engage mathematicians when they do mathematics. We consistently deliver the following message to students: "Do only what makes sense to you and persist until it does."

About the Lessons in This Book

The book is organized into two sections. The six chapters in Part I describe lessons that integrate ideas from different strands of the math curriculum. Each chapter describes instruction that ranges in length from one to eight class periods. Some of the lessons deal with areas of mathematics that usually don't receive a great deal of attention in the middle-school curriculum, such as probability, statistics, and logical reasoning. Others present new ways to deal with more traditional topics, including number, algebra, and measurement. All lessons illustrate how a problem-solving approach in all areas of the math curriculum can translate into classroom instruction.

Part II presents two units of instruction. Chapter 7 presents a two-to-three week unit of study about the area of circles. The unit integrates geometry, measurement, and number. Traditionally, students learn the standard formula— $A = \pi r^2$—for finding the area of a circle. They learn about the derivation of the formula, memorize it, apply it in many examples, and are tested on its use. This unit takes a broader approach. It involves students in an exploration of various methods for approximating the area of a circle. Along with presenting the content of the lessons, the chapter explains how to organize the unit, introduce the activities to the class, structure the students' recording, and process the activities in whole class discussions. In addition, the chapter addresses the issue of grading students' work in a unit that emphasizes students' thinking and reasoning, not merely getting correct answers.

Chapter 8 focuses on percents, another topic basic to the middle-school mathematics curriculum. Though the primary focus is percents, the lessons also provide students experiences with ideas about geometry, measurement, and statistics. The intent of the instruction is to involve students actively in making sense of percents for themselves and thereby constructing their own understanding. As with the unit about finding the areas of circles, the lessons in this unit may be grouped together for a continuous span of instruction. However, different from the investigation of area, the lessons in this unit do not contribute to one specific exploration. The lessons present percents in a variety of settings and therefore can be spread over time to provide students experience with percents throughout the year.

We introduce all lessons with a rationale that presents issues we'd like teachers to consider. Throughout the vignettes, we continue to comment and expand on the issues in the contexts of what occurred in the particular classroom lessons. Finally, we reflect on each lesson to provide a conclusion that addresses the underlying issues once again. Most important, all lessons in the book model classroom instruction for which students' thinking and reasoning are the main priorities.

Questions from Teachers

Teachers have reported that the lessons are beneficial. They've said that they enjoy teaching them, that they find their students respond positively and are eager for more.

Teachers have also reported teaching issues that concern them. We've received the following questions and comments:

"I wish I knew how all these activities fit together. Are there some which should precede others?"

"I understand why these lessons are valuable for students, but they take a great deal of time."

"If I do these lessons, what do I leave out of my traditional program? How can I integrate them with my textbook and district curriculum guide?"

"My classes are grouped by ability. Are these lessons suited for all students or just for students at some levels?"

"I know problem solving is important, but I still have to answer to the tests. How do I do both?"

"How much time should I spend on the basic skills?"

"What do I do about giving grades?"

"How can I use manipulative materials? Will the students think they're baby stuff?"

"What if the students did the activity the year before? Will they be bored or disappointed?"

"My students enjoy these lessons, but are they learning what they need?"

"What do I need to do to plan and organize an entire year of instruction?"

We don't offer definitive answers to all these questions. Quite honestly, we're continually searching to clarify our thinking and to frame answers that communicate to teachers and relate to classroom realities. What we've done in this collection of lessons is share what we've tried with students, what we've learned from our experiences, and what we've come to believe as a result. And since what we've learned has evolved from our classroom teaching experiences, our responses to the questions posed are embedded in the vignettes of lessons we've actually taught to middle-school students.

Linking Assessment and Instruction

A note about assessment in the classroom. In our view, there is no substantive difference between learning experiences and assessment measures. Classroom experiences that present students with problem situations that are new, usually complex, and often ambiguous can simultaneously serve students' learning and our assessment of their progress. Students' work when facing such problems reveals a great deal about their understanding while it contributes to the development, enhancement, and deepening of their learning. When we do give quizzes or tests, we give the message to students that we are going to take a special look at the results with an eye to assessing their progress. But, in fact, we're doing that all the time.

We do find that when we give quizzes and tests, students react differently. They sit taller. They face the task with more seriousness than they bring to usual classroom work. They feel that their work "really" counts, a response that the culture of their school experience to date has reinforced. We work to change this, so that both class assignments and quizzes "really" count but in different ways. It's like the difference between performing a piano piece for the teacher during a lesson and performing that same piece at a recital. Both provide the opportunity for feedback that can contribute toward improvement, but the settings are different and therefore the experience is different.

The idea of performance is key, both to learning and assessing, whether at the music lesson or in math class. Learning an instrument calls for being a musician. At the same time children learn exercises, practice scales, and work at arpeggios, they play songs and learn new pieces. Never at a recital are students expected to show proficiency with scales or arpeggios; rather, they're expected to show their abilities as musicians at whatever their level of competence.

We view student learning of mathematics in the same way. Students learn procedures and develop skills when they study mathematics, such as how to name fractions, how to measure with a ruler, how to figure percents. But we want them to learn procedures and skills in the context of doing mathematics, for the purpose of thinking through situations and solving problems. Even though students sometimes practice procedures and skills in isolation, their proficiency with them is in no way equated with or mistaken for being proficient in mathematics.

How to Use This Book

Just as students' learning in the classroom is supported when they have the opportunity to interact and exchange ideas, so will your planning and teaching be supported through discussion with colleagues. We found it beneficial when writing this book to plan together, try the lessons with different classes, talk about what happened, make changes, and try again. Rarely were we completely satisfied after teaching a lesson for the first time. Lessons always cried out for tinkering, both in the content of the mathematics and the management of the classroom.

The versions of lessons presented in the book are ones that worked the best, and they are offered as starting places for your planning. Be sure to keep in mind that the students in your classes will respond differently from those described. Also, your teaching style may be different from ours. There's no one way to help students learn mathematics. And there's no one best way for any of these lessons to be taught.

For additional help in planning, some of the lessons can be seen in the three-part videotape series, *Mathematics for Middle School*, available from Cuisenaire Company of America. Parts of Chapters 1, 2, 5, 6, and 8 are shown. In some instances, the lesson described in the book was taught to the class shown on the videotape. In others, the lesson described in the book was taught to a different class. In either case, watching the lessons on videotape provides further information about each lesson. A reference is included in each chapter for which a videotaped version is available.

In Conclusion

Teaching is hard. Teaching middle-school students is especially hard. It's a tender and vulnerable time of life for these students. They're in the midst of many changes—physical, emotional, and intellectual—and their needs are compelling.

The time schedules of middle schools are also demanding. Middle schools are usually organized so instructional periods range from forty minutes to an hour. Teachers generally see five classes each day, often with only a three-minute passing time between periods. It's a complicated environment in which students and teachers are in constant motion.

With the reality of time schedules and students' differences, we've worked to find ways to make math classes interesting, engaging, and valuable for students. We understand and respect the enormity of the task and have tried to address the needs of teachers while also addressing the needs of students. We hope that what we've learned will provide help for others struggling to do a challenging job in the best way possible.

A LOGICAL REASONING ACTIVITY

The *Curriculum and Evaluation Standards* of the National Council of Teachers of Mathematics (1989) states: "Reasoning is fundamental to the knowing and doing of mathematics. . . . Conjecturing and demonstrating the logical validity of conjecture are the essence of the creative act of doing mathematics" (p. 81). This chapter describes Riddles with Color Tiles, an activity that models a lesson that answers this standard.

Solving and creating riddles with Color Tiles engages students in making conjectures, testing them, and listening to and evaluating the ideas of others. The students in this eighth-grade class were given series of clues to determine the number and color of tiles in a bag. They then worked in pairs and wrote riddles of their own, creating sequences of clues to lead unquestionably to a particular collection of tiles. Finally, they solved other students' riddles.

The lessons were taught near the beginning of the school year. The students had little previous experience with manipulatives in their math learning, and the activity provided them with an introduction to using materials. The students had no experience with cooperative groups, and this activity gave them an opportunity to work collaboratively. Also, these students' math learning had been concentrated on arithmetic, and this lesson gave them experience with a mathematics activity that had reasoning as its goal rather than computing.

Four class periods were spent on the riddle activities. As it was early in the year, the lessons were equally geared toward dealing with class management and social issues and math issues. Generally the students were a cheerful group but rather unruly. The class was orderly in a lecture situation or when doing individual seatwork but had no experience learning math through an activity approach. The lesson was a challenge—and well worth the effort.

Videotape   "Riddles with Color Tiles" appears in Part 3 of *Mathematics for Middle School*. The videotaped lesson was taught to a class of seventh graders in two class periods. On the first day, the students solved riddles using clues presented by the teacher. In the next day's class, the students worked in pairs to create their own riddles.

Day 1

I began by showing the class a plastic bag of Color Tiles. "I've put some of these kinds of tiles in each of these two paper bags," I said. I then showed the class the two bags, pointing out that I had labeled them Riddle 1 and Riddle 2.

"I've also prepared clues to help you figure out what tiles I put in each of these bags," I said. "What I'm going to do is give you some tiles to use during class. Then, as I give you clues, you'll use the tiles to figure out what I've put in the bag."

The students had no experience with the tiles, so I knew they would need time with them before I continued the lesson. "Because you're not familiar with these tiles," I explained to the class, "I'm going to give you the chance to explore with them before I ask for your attention to continue with the lesson and solve the riddles." I had prepared 12 small plastic bags for pairs of students to share. There were 80 tiles in each bag, 20 each of red, blue, green, and yellow. I organized the class into partners by having students slide their desks next to each other. There was one group of three.

The students' free exploration went predictably. Most built towers or lined up the tiles in rows to knock over as with dominoes. Some built checkerboard arrays of squares and rectangles. Some created other patterns. One boy used the tiles to spell his name. The students were noisy but involved. I circulated and observed. I also talked to those students who seemed to think it was a keen idea to jiggle others' desks to make towers topple.

After about ten minutes, I brought the class to attention. "I know that you're still interested in playing with the tiles," I said, "but I want you to stop now so I can begin the math activity. Please dismantle your towers and domino rows and put the tiles in one pile. Leave a clear space in front of you where you can put tiles that follow the directions I'm going to give." Getting their attention was difficult. It took several more announcements from me before all students followed these directions. Finally I felt I had their focus off the tiles and on me.

I wrote the first clue on the board:

Clue 1. There are fewer than 15 tiles.

"Using this information," I said, "show with the tiles one possibility of what might be in the bag." Some chaos erupted. Actually, the chaos was just about total. Some students followed the directions immediately. Others worked more slowly. Still others were confused and unsure what they were supposed to do. A few of the students reached for paper and pencil to write their answers. Some appeared not to have heard what I had said and started again to build towers or set up domino patterns with the tiles. The room became noisy as students began to talk, some with their partners and some with friends across the room. I circulated, getting students back on track. When I had their attention again, I repeated the directions.

"I understand that this is new for you," I said. "Listen again so you learn to follow my directions. You don't need paper and pencil. Show me with the tiles what you think can possibly be in the bag. As I give you additional clues, you'll show how your ideas change by changing the arrangement of tiles on your desk. I should be able to see clearly on one area of your desk what you think might be in the bag." After about a minute, every student had displayed a collection of fewer than 15 tiles.

Then I wrote the next clue:

Clue 2. I used two colors.

There was a slight scramble for different tiles but less chaos and confusion with this clue. I circulated quickly through the room to check. Most students had made adjustments to their first tile arrangements.

I wrote the third clue on the board:

Clue 3. There are no green or red tiles.

The situation improved further. All students made their adjustments quickly.

"What do you know now for sure?" I asked.

Several hands went up. "There are blues and yellows," Chris said.

"There are less than 15," Tami said.

"You don't have any red or green tiles," Andy added.

"There are less than 15," Jason said. Some kids laughed. I ignored their response and decided not to point out to Jason how listening could help him avoid repeating what someone had already reported.

I called on Sinead. "You can't tell for sure yet," she said.

"I'll give another clue," I said, and wrote on the board:

Clue 4. I have twice as many blue tiles as yellow tiles.

This clue narrowed the solution to four possibilities.

When all students had an arrangement displayed on their desks, I asked for someone to report what he or she thought could be in the bag. Hasani raised his hand.

"6 blue and 3 yellow," he reported. I wrote on the board:

B	Y
6	3

"Does anyone have a different idea?" I asked. Jesse reported, "4 blue and 2 yellow." I added this to the chart.

B	Y
6	3
4	2

"Any other ideas?" I asked. Only boys had their hands raised. I called on Michael and added his suggestion to my list.

B	Y
6	3
4	2
2	1

I continued. Still no girls had volunteered. I called on Steven and recorded his arrangement. "It's already up there," Robert said. Steven nodded and I erased it.

Clue #1: There are fewer than 15 tiles.

Clue #2: I used two colors.

Clue #3: There are no green or red tiles.

Clue #4: I have twice as many blue tiles as yellow.

B	Y
6	3
4	2

After being given the fourth clue, the students report the possible solutions.

Zack offered a different suggestion. I added it to the list.

B	Y
6	3
4	2
2	1
8	4

There were no other suggestions.
I then wrote the fifth clue:

Clue 5. There are 3 more blues than yellows.

This was the deciding piece of information. It was obvious to the students that there were 6 blue tiles and 3 yellow tiles in the bag. I asked the class if they needed to see the tiles in the bag. No one thought that was necessary.

"We already know what's in there," Chris said. Nods indicated that his opinion expressed the general view.

I then pressed on with the second riddle. "For the second riddle," I told the class, "I'm going to give you the first three clues all together." Doing this would give the students more information to analyze at one time. I felt this would give me the chance to circulate and see what they were doing. Also, it would narrow the possibilities more quickly.

Clue 1. There are 10 tiles.
Clue 2. I used three colors.
Clue 3. I have zero yellow tiles.

Students displayed their possibilities fairly quickly this time. Rather than the confusion that was apparent when I gave the first clues for the other riddle, this time the students understood the idea of using the tiles to show their thinking about the clues.

"When I give the fourth clue," I said, "you and your partner are to work together. You are to show not just one possibility but all the possible arrangements that fit the information." I had chosen a riddle that would allow each pair enough tiles to build all the arrangements. I wrote the fourth clue on the board:

Clue 4. I have the same number of green and blue tiles.

I circulated while the students worked, getting a few of the pairs on track, clarifying for others. The class was going more smoothly now. The noise level was lower and the concentration more complete. I attributed this to two factors. With this second riddle, the students were more comfortable with what they were expected to do. Also, because they felt they could do it, they were more willing to stay involved.

I called the class back to attention. "Can someone tell me one arrangement that fits the clues?" I asked. Now two girls raised their hands along with eight boys. I called on Aneitra and recorded her suggestion.

R	G	B
4	3	3

Halbert described an arrangement that was not a possibility. "1 red, 5 green, and 5 blue," he said. I recorded as he reported each color.

R	G	B
4	3	3
1	5	5

I handled the discrepancy by saying, "I think your possibility violates one of the clues. Who can figure out which one it violates?"

Halbert figured it out for himself. "Oh, yeah," he said, "I have more than 10 tiles." I erased his suggestion.

I continued recording their suggestions, arranging them so that the numbers of reds were given in descending order. All four possibilities were reported.

R	G	B
8	1	1
6	2	2
4	3	3
2	4	4

I then gave the fifth clue. I wrote:

Clue 5. There are more red than green or blue tiles.

"That doesn't tell us the answer," Jason blurted out.
"What does it tell you?" I asked. About half the hands shot up.

"It can't be 2 reds," Zack said, "because that wouldn't be enough." The others agreed, and I crossed out that possibility.

"Does the fifth clue eliminate anything else?" I asked. Heads nodded no.

"The sixth clue is the deciding one," I then said. "Before I write it on the board, however, I want to give you a chance to guess what it is. I'll tell you what I actually put in the bag. There are 4 red, 3 green, and 3 blue." I circled that possibility on my chart.

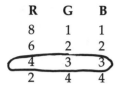

R	G	B
8	1	1
6	2	2
4	3	3
2	4	4

"What clue might get that result?" I asked.

Several had suggestions. "You could have said that there was one more red than blue," Tri said. I wrote Tri's suggestion on the board. Taking the time to write it gave the others time to consider it.

"I agree that that would work," I said, "but that's not the clue I had in mind."

"It could say, 'There are 4 red,'" Tami said.

I wrote Tami's suggestion on the board and said, "That would work, but it's not what I was thinking of."

I called on Steven. "If you add the greens and blues, then you have two more than the reds," he offered. I wrote Steven's suggestion on the board. It wasn't my clue either.

"These are all workable clues," I told the class. "Actually, there are many different clues that will produce the same solution. Here's the sixth clue I made up." I wrote on the board:

Clue 6. There are ¾ as many green as red tiles.

This clue elicited a few groans about fractions.

"I have three more questions to ask you about this riddle," I said to the class. "First of all, are there any clues I included that you didn't need to solve the riddle, that aren't really necessary?" The room was now quiet.

Zack raised his hand. "You didn't need clue number 3, because the three colors you used are mentioned later."

Jason said, "I don't think you need clue 2 either, because you can figure that out from clue 5." Zack nodded agreement.

"But I think those clues helped us solve it," Sinead said.

"Yeah, but you didn't have to have them," Jason insisted.

"I agree with both of you," I said. "Those clues may be helpful, but they aren't essential. There is a word that describes information that is extra and not necessary. The word is *redundant*." I wrote the word on the board but didn't say any more about it. I planned to return to the idea in a few days.

"Here's another question," I continued. "How come only even numbers of red tiles are listed in the possibilities?"

Jesse had an answer to this one. "Because green and blue are the same," he said, "and if you take those away from 10, you can't get an odd number."

"Does anyone have another way to express that?" I asked.

Robert did. "If red was odd, then green and blue couldn't be the same," he said.

"Any other ideas?" I asked. There weren't any.

"One more question. Do you think it makes any difference what order I give the clues in?" I asked.

I waited a bit, but no one volunteered an answer to this. I didn't comment or press further. It was now near the end of the period. I had the students put the tiles back in the bags and dismissed the class.

Day 2

My plan for the second class was to have the students work with their partners to write riddles.

"If you were going to make up a riddle like the ones I presented yesterday," I began, "what might you do to get started?"

I called on Jeremy. "You'd probably put some tiles in a bag," he said.

"Yes, that's actually what I did first," I responded. I wrote on the board:

1. Put some tiles in the bag.

"What might you do next?" I asked.

Robert answered. "You should think of a clue that gives some information but doesn't give it away," he said. I wrote on the board:

2. Write a clue that gives information but doesn't give it away.

"What next?" I asked.

"Write more clues," Jesse offered. I added this to the list:

3. Write more clues.

"Now what?" I continued. There were no hands raised. I tried another question.

"How do you think I decided when I had written enough clues?" I asked.

Jesse raised his hand. "You tested them?" he offered tentatively.

"Yes," I responded, "I tested them by using the tiles just as you did yesterday with the two riddles I presented. I wanted to be sure my clues produced a solution. I also wanted to be sure my clues produced only one answer." I wrote on the board:

4. Test the clues to be sure they produce exactly one solution.

"Today, you are going to work together to write clues for a riddle," I continued. "I'll give you and your partner a paper bag and tiles. You are to follow the steps I listed on the board. For your riddles, use no more than 15 tiles. Also, write your names on the paper bag as well as on your paper."

"A couple more directions," I added. "When you and your partner feel you need help, raise your hands to call me. Also, when you've written and tested your riddle, raise your hands, and I'll come and check that it works."

I knew that their brief time for free exploration the day before had not been enough to satisfy their curiosity, and I planned for this as well. "Before you get started on your riddle," I said, "I want to give you some more time to explore with the tiles. I know that some of you are still curious about them. Here's how I'd like you to handle this. It's now 9:35. Begin work on your riddle no later than 9:45. I'll remind you when you should be working on the clues if you haven't kept track of the time."

Michael and Juliette work together to write a riddle.

I had them get into their groups while two students passed out the tiles and bags. I assigned Tammy, who had been absent the day before, to work with Rachel and Tami. I also wrote on the board:

9:35   Explore
9:45   Begin writing clues

I've gotten in the habit of writing the directions that I give verbally on the board. I think it's a helpful reminder for some of the students. For others, it's essential. Their attention gets distracted easily and often during class, and they miss a great deal of what I say and ask. Besides, I'm giving a lot of specific directions for them to follow. If the directions are on the chalkboard, students have a way to check what they are to do when they get overwhelmed or confused.

Building time into the lesson for the students to explore with the tiles was successful. I had to remind only one pair when it was time to begin work on writing clues. Some of the students began to work on their riddles before 9:45. This was good, because it helped stagger their requests for assistance.

I had no idea how much time students would need to write riddles. The class period ended at 10:10, and I needed at least five minutes at the end of class to collect their papers and the materials and to talk with them. This left about fifteen minutes for them to work. Some finished in less time but were interested enough to start another riddle.

I was busy during these fifteen minutes. Some students wanted reassurance that their first clues were OK. I responded by telling them whether their clues made sense to me or, if they didn't, why they didn't. Others wanted me to mediate disagreements with their partners. My response was to tell them they had to work it out together. Some students wanted me to check their completed riddles. Before I would do so, I asked if they had checked that their clues worked by trying to solve the riddle with the tiles. If they hadn't, I asked them to do that first before I tried it.

When I checked riddles, I solved them with the tiles. For about half the riddles I checked, the students' clues produced more than one possible solution. For example, Robert and Halbert called me over to check their riddle. They had written:

1. *I have more than 3 and less than 14.*
2. *I have all four colors.*
3. *I have three times as many reds as yellows.*
4. *I have more blues than reds and more reds than yellow.*

I worked with the tiles, explaining as I worked what I was doing. I put out one of each color. "That satisfies clue number 2," I said, "but I have to add more reds to take care of clue number 3. If I add 2 more reds, then I have 3 reds and 1 of each of the others. That works. But then clue 4 says that I have to have more blues than reds and more reds than yellows. I already have more reds than yellows, so that's OK. If I add 3 more blues, then I'll have enough blues. I have 3 reds, 4 blues, 1 yellow, and 1 green, and that's 9 altogether, which fits clue number 1."

I looked at the boys. "How did I do?" I asked.

"You didn't get it right," Halbert said. "That's not what we have in the bag."

"But I followed your clues," I said.

"She did," Robert said to Halbert.

"What do we do now?" Halbert asked.

"One thing you can do," I answered, "is add more clues so you eliminate possibilities such as mine and narrow it down so only what you have in the bag works."

I left them. When they handed in their riddle, a fifth clue was included: *"I have the same amount of greens and blues."*

I interrupted their work just after 10:00. Each group had a riddle to hand in, though I didn't have the chance to check all their clues during the class. I collected the riddles and the tiles and had the students put their desks back in order. By 10:05, I had their attention.

I used the remaining class time to give the students feedback on the activity and to hear from them. "I was interested in the variety of clues I read in the riddles I checked," I said. "The ones I didn't check, I'll get to tomorrow. Also, tomorrow you'll have the chance to read and solve other people's riddles, and I'll explain then how we'll do that."

"I have a question for you," I continued. "How do you feel about working together compared to working alone?"

Their responses were positive. "You have someone to talk with." "You get more ideas that way." "You have help." "It's more fun."

"These are some of the reasons I think it's valuable for you to work with each other," I said. "I have two concerns, however. Sometimes it got too noisy, and I had to ask you to quiet down. I think you can do better by paying attention to

(*left*) Sinead and Krystal's clues lead to one solution. (*right*) Halbert and Robert added a fifth clue to make their riddle work.

the level of your voices, and I'll be looking for that improvement tomorrow. Also, sometimes I think you ask me for help before you talk it over yourselves. Remember, you have to try to solve a problem together before calling on me for help." It was then time for recess, and I dismissed the class.

The class had gone fairly well. I think this was because the activity was the right level for the students. They felt they could tackle the task and were also intrigued by it. Too, having each other's support contributed to their comfort and willingness to work.

That night, in preparation for the next day, I stapled each of their riddles to their paper bags. (I could have had them do this in class, but I hadn't given them that instruction.) In addition, I wrote a riddle for them to try that led to more than one possible solution and also had a redundant clue.

Day 3

As the students were entering the room, I wrote on the chalkboard clues I'd written the night before.

1. I have fewer than 15 tiles.
2. I have three colors.
3. I have twice as many yellow tiles as blue tiles.
4. There are two colors with the same number of tiles.
5. I have the same number of yellow and red tiles.

I had the students get into their groups and distributed the tiles. Then I called their attention to the chalkboard.

"This riddle needs some more work," I said. "It has a problem because the clues lead to more than one solution, not just one. See if you can figure out what's wrong with it. Also, see which clues you think are not needed at all." I was saying this to prepare them for solving the riddles they had devised.

This part of the lesson did not go as smoothly as I would have liked. Some figured out the problem with the riddle quickly and had to wait for others who worked more slowly. Still others were fooling with the tiles rather than attending to the task. (I was living through the beginning-of-the-year growing pains when many organizational problems are not yet resolved.)

When everyone had made some progress on analyzing the riddle, I called the class back to attention and led a discussion of the clues. I asked for possible solutions and listed the two that were suggested:

R	Y	B
2	2	1
4	4	2

I told the students that I had put 4 red, 4 yellow, and 2 blue tiles in the bag and asked for suggestions on how to change the clues so they would produce exactly this arrangement.

"You could say that you had more than 5 tiles," Krystal suggested.

"You could write that you used 10 tiles," Andy said.

"It could say you have between 6 and 12 tiles," Robert offered.

I added to the first clue on the board to model for the students how they might alter the riddles they would be solving.

1. I have fewer than 15 tiles and a greater number than 5 tiles.
2. I have three colors.
3. I have twice as many yellow tiles as blue tiles.
4. There are two colors with the same number of tiles.
5. I have the same number of yellow and red tiles.

Then I asked about unnecessary clues. Students had different thoughts, but there was some agreement that clues 2 and 4 were not necessary. It was difficult for many of the students to explain their reasoning. They couldn't find words. I believe that time and experience will help with this.

I then told the students that they would be solving others' riddles. "For each riddle you solve," I said, "work together, but you each record in your own notebook. After you solve a riddle, check your solution by looking in the bag. Also, when recording your work for each riddle, I want you to use the format I've written on the board." I showed them how to structure their work:

```
Date:
Riddle by:
Solution:

☐ Too Easy  ☐ Just Right  ☐ Too Hard
Explanation:

Redundant Clues:
```

I also gave more explicit instructions for their explanations. "Describe how you figured out the solution," I said. "Include your thoughts about which clues were most helpful, what confusion you experienced, and which clues you feel could be improved." I wrote these points on the board.

"In the space for redundant clues," I said, "list the clues you think could be eliminated and explain why."

> 1. I Have 15 tiles
>
> 2. I Have three colors
>
> 3. red + yellow = 10 tiles
>
> 4. there are no blue tiles
>
> 5. there are 2 more green than red. Red than green. A.S.
>
> 6. The green tiles plus the yellow tiles = the red amount plus one

Alesia revised Jesse and Zack's riddle and initialed her changes.

I gave a few last procedural directions. "All the riddles are on the back table," I said. "To begin, you may want to choose your own riddle first to check it further or have me check it. When you finish with a riddle, return it to the table. Also, an important last direction. If you think the riddle you're working on has a problem, go to the students who wrote it, discuss it, and edit it together. I'll help if you need me."

They all got involved. The students interacted freely. The room was noisy, but it was the purposeful hum of work going on. I still had to talk to some of the

> Solution 8G 4R 2y 1B
> ☑ Too Easy, ☐ Just Right, ☐ Too Hard
> Explanation
>   Clue 3, 4, and 5 works. First I got one of each color, then then I put twice as many yellow as blue then twice as many green than red. then I subtracted 10 34-10 19. then I put out 8 green.
>
> Redundant
>   Clue 1 was redundant "We have all the colors" because of clue 3 "I have twice as many yellow as blue and twice as many green as red" clue 2 was redundant "We have more than one tile"

> Solution
>   4 green, 3 yellow, 2 blue and 1 red
>
> ☐ TOO EASY ☒ JUST RIGHT ☐ TOO HARD
>
> EXPLANATION: 8+3+5 helped. We just went through all the clues and it worked out very well.
> None of the clues could be improved, None at all.
>
> Redundant Clues—
> Number 2 you could have done without.

Students solved and analyzed each other's riddles.

students about sticking to the task, but the improvement in their attention to their work was noticeable.

The weakest parts of their written work were their explanations. For the redundant clues, for example, though most students were able to identify them, most did not attempt to explain why they were unnecessary. "I don't know what to say" was a common response when I probed. I plan to continue to give them more class experience with explaining their reasoning and look for improvement over time with assignments of this kind.

After the students had worked for twenty minutes, I interrupted them to give them time to clean up and give them a homework assignment. I felt they had enough experience to be able to do a riddle problem at home individually. I posted the assignment for them:

Write clues for a collection of tiles with 1 red, 1 blue, 3 green, and 6 yellow. Follow these directions:

1. Use lined paper.

2. Date your paper.

3. Write complete sentences.

4. Number your clues.

I was interested in the variety of clues they would write for the same collection of tiles. I planned to use their homework to begin the next day's class.

Day 4

When the students arrived in class, I settled them into their groups and explained how I was going to deal with the homework. "I'm going to come around and check that you've done your assignment," I said, "but I'm not going to collect it yet. Before you hand it in, you are to compare your riddles and check that they work. See if any clues can be improved or eliminated. Make corrections together. When you're satisfied, sign each other's work; then hand it in. After you do this, return to solving others' riddles."

Handling homework in this way was new for students. Though they had had experience correcting each other's papers, they weren't used to collaborating to check each other's work. I was using their homework as a means to further their learning through cooperative interaction. It went well.

Five students hadn't done the homework. Going around while the class began working gave me a chance to talk to them and find out what the problems were. I got the usual collection of reasons: "I had a headache." "My sister had a birthday party." "I went to my visit my grandma." "I just forgot." I explained that I would give them a zero in my book for their homework that day, but that they still were to work with their partners and sign off on their assignments. I didn't want their not doing an assignment to be an impediment to learning in class. I also told them I expected them to hand in their riddles the next day.

The class went smoothly. Again, I interrupted the students in time to give them their homework; this time the assignment was prepared as a handout. I asked the students to write a letter about their experiences with the riddles. I was interested in their reaction to the four-day experience. I told them to use

clue 1: There are four colors.

clue 2: There are twice as many yellow than green.

clue 3: Yellow is an even number.

clue 4: There are eleven tiles.

clue 5: There are the same number of reds as there are of blue.

clue 6: Two of the colors have only one tile each.

clue 7: Red is one of the colors described in clue 6.

---

clue 1 I have less than fifteen tiles

clue 2 I have more than 10

clue 3 I have twice as many yellow as green.

clue 4 I have 4 colors in the bag.

clue 5 I have the same of red and blue

clue 6 I have 3 green ~~yellow~~ tiles

clue 7 Subtract ⚖ from the ~~green~~ and you have the number of red and blue.

Clue #1- I Have 4 colors

Clue #2- Red+blue = $\frac{1}{3}$ of the yellow tiles

Clue #3- I have less than 15 tiles.

Clue #4- Green is half of yellow.

Clue #5.- All tiles added together is a prime number.

For homework, students wrote clues for a collection of tiles with 1 red, 1 blue, 3 green, and 6 yellow.

Dear Ms. Burns

I think the thing your doing with the color tiles is good because your teaching different types of math in a fun way. When we first started out doing it I thought it would be hard but know that I'm use to it and know how to do it I like it and I do recommend you do it with other classes. There is nothing wrong with the way you do it but you should add more colors and make it more interesting.

Dear Ms Burns,

I enjoyed your project on the chips. It not only made us solve problems but make them too, and I like doing that.

In the project I mostly used deduction until you came to the last number.

Yes I recommend you do this with other classes I'm sure they would enjoy it because it's different then what is usualy taught in a math class.

I have no suggestions for improvement to offer you

Having students write about their experiences gives insights into their views about what they study.

proper letter form and to be sure to answer the questions I had written on the assignment sheet. The questions were:

Did you enjoy the activity? Why or why not?

What math skills did you use?

Would you recommend I teach this to other classes? Why?

What suggestions for improving the lesson can you offer?

For the time being, this was the last day I planned to work on riddles in class. However, I intended to return to the riddles later in the year and use clues that included other math concepts, such as fractions, percents, ratios, primes, palindromes, powers, and square numbers. For now, this seemed like enough.

Final Thoughts

I noticed changes over the four days in class. As the students became interested in the activity and felt more confident with the work I presented, they became clearer about their responsibility. They settled down and became more purposeful toward their work.

There is general consensus that students ought to be active learners in math class. They should be exploring complex problems, using concrete materials, working cooperatively in small groups, and writing about and discussing their ideas. Teachers sometimes tell me: "Yes, it sounds good, but it won't work with my class." The implication is that the abilities of the students or their behavior (or perhaps both) are deterrents to implementing these recommendations.

I know that some classes are more difficult to manage than others. I know that some students have more difficulty learning than others. Still, I don't think these reasons are sufficient to avoid the activities. All students deserve the opportunity to explore, conjecture, reason logically, and use a variety of mathematical methods and materials to solve problems. Even with the frustrations I experienced in the lessons, I also had my rewards and feel that this kind of teaching is clearly worth it.

INTRODUCING ALGEBRA

Students often get their first glimpse of algebra from older sisters or brothers. The math papers they see are filled with more letters than numbers and seem very mysterious. Students are generally impressed and curious; some are a bit fearful.

For some students, algebra classes unlock the mystery of this new subject. These students learn to solve equations easily. They like the orderliness of procedures, enjoy solving word problems, and feel satisfied when they get to the final $x =$.

Other students have different reactions. All teachers who have taught algebra have encountered students who report, "I don't get it." "This is dumb" is another common reaction. Students who do not take pleasure in the orderly procedures ask, "What's it good for anyway?"

For many students, important elements are missing from algebra instruction. They don't learn how algebra fits with the rest of the mathematics they've been studying. They focus on the various procedures and problems to be solved and pay attention to the rules and rituals of algebra while ignoring its place in the world of mathematics.

This chapter explains how algebra was introduced to a class of eighth graders. The five-day investigation integrated algebra with geometry and arithmetic. Each student was given a 10-by-10 grid of squared-centimeter paper and asked to figure the number of squares in its border. After describing and comparing their different methods, the students solved the same problem for grids of other sizes. Finally, they generalized their methods of calculation into algebraic formulas. By introducing algebra as an extension of arithmetic and geometry, the students were helped to see algebra as connected to their previous math learning.

Videotape The "Border Problem" appears in Part 3 of *Mathematics for Middle School*. The videotaped lesson was taught to a class of seventh and eighth graders. After several students present their methods for figuring out the border of the 10-by-10 grid, they test their methods on a 5-by-5 grid. The class is then shown a larger grid and asked to describe how they'd figure out its border. Finally, they work in pairs to translate their methods into algebraic formulas.

Day 1

"What do you know about algebra?" I asked the class.

I was interested in learning what these eighth graders knew or had heard about algebra. My question was met with general silence. Finally, Jesse raised his hand.

"It has to do with using letters to stand for numbers," he said.

"Yes," I responded, "letters are often used for numbers in algebra. Does anyone have a different idea?"

Zack raised his hand. "You have to solve for unknowns," he said.

No other students had ideas to offer.

I then wrote on the chalkboard:

Algebra is a generalization of arithmetic.

"What is arithmetic?" I asked.

Lots of hands went up to answer this question. "It has to do with numbers." "It's addition and subtraction and like that." "It's multiplication and division, too." "You do things to numbers and get answers." "You do it with whole numbers and fractions and decimals."

I gave all the students who raised their hands the chance to contribute. Then I asked another question, "What is a generalization?"

Fewer hands went up. "It's the opposite of *specific*," Chris said.

"It's like those statements we write about graphs," Krystal said.

"They're conclusions," Jeremy added.

"In order to help you learn about algebra," I then said to the class, "I'm going to start from what you already know. I'm going to give you a problem you can solve using arithmetic. Then I'll introduce you to how to use algebra to generalize your solutions. We won't get to the algebra part today; instead, we'll focus just on the problem."

In general, students learn from connecting new experiences to what they know. I want students to see algebra in relation to what they've already learned, not as a topic separate from the mathematics they've been studying.

I had cut a ten-by-ten grid from squared-centimeter paper for each student. I distributed the grids at this point and asked the students to find out how many squares were on the grid. It was easy for them to figure there were 100 squares.

I had colored in a border on my grid, one row of squares around the outside. "Now I'd like you to find out how many squares there are in the border of your grid," I said, "the row all around the outer edge."

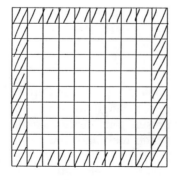

There were murmurs as the students worked. "I know, it's 40." "It's got to be 40." "I'll count to check." "Hey, it's not 40." "Oops, I'd better count again." "I got 36." "Yeah, I got 36, too." "You could have fooled me."

When all the students had convinced themselves that there were 36 squares in the border, I asked for volunteers to explain how they figured it.

I called on Jason. "I did 10 times 4," he said, "and then I subtracted 4 and got 36."

"Why do you think your method makes sense?" I asked.

"Because you can't count the corners twice," Jason answered, "so I subtracted them at the end."

I recorded Jason's method on the board numerically.

$$\begin{array}{r} 10 \\ \times\ 4 \\ \hline 40 \\ -\ 4 \\ \hline 36 \end{array}$$

"Did anyone do it a different way?" I asked.

Robert had a suggestion. "I counted the sides and added," he said. "The top has 10, then the next side has 9 because you already counted the corner, and the next side has 9, and the last side has 8 because you counted both corners."

Robert and Steven figure out how many squares there are in the border of the grid.

I recorded Robert's method on the board.

$$
\begin{array}{r}
10 \\
9 \\
9 \\
+8 \\
\hline
36
\end{array}
$$

"Any other way?" I asked.

Tami reported next. "I just multiplied 9 times 4," she said.

"Why does that make sense?" I asked.

"Because I didn't want to count the corners twice," Tami answered. "I just said that each side gets one corner, so they each have 9 squares, and I multiplied that by 4."

I numerically recorded Tami's method on the board. Then I asked, "Any other ideas?"

I called on Zack. "There are 64 squares in the middle," he said, "because that's 8 times 8. I subtracted 64 from 100 and got 36."

I added Zack's method to the board. "Another way?" I asked.

Chris had an idea. "I added 10 and 10 for the top and bottom," he said. "Then there are only 8 left on each side, so add 8 and 8, and you get 36."

I recorded Chris's idea on the board. "Another idea?" I asked again. There were no more volunteers.

"I have another method," I said. "I'll write it on the board numerically and then see if someone can explain what I was thinking." I wrote:

$$
\begin{array}{r}
8 \\
\times 4 \\
\hline
32 \\
+4 \\
\hline
36
\end{array}
$$

Several hands shot up. I called on Juliette. "You took out the corners first and then added them back in at the end," she said.

"Where does the 8 come from?" I asked.

Steven answered. "That's how much is on each edge without the corners," he said.

I now had six methods recorded on the chalkboard:

1	2	3	4	5	6
10	10	9	100	10	8
×4	9	×4	−64	10	×4
40	9	36	36	8	32
−4	+8			+8	+4
36	36			36	36

I then gave the students a writing assignment to do. "Choose one of the methods for solving the border problem," I said. "Describe it in your notebook so that someone who wasn't in class would have a way to find the answer. Be sure to explain why the method works."

Having the students write helps them find out what they know and what they don't know. Also, their writing gives me insights into their understanding. I knew that writing was difficult for many of the students in the class. They had not had much previous experience with writing about their thinking processes in their math classes.

When I read through their explanations that night, I found most to be very poor, both in the thoughts they expressed and the grammar they used. The following are samples from about half the students.

Michael wrote: *You can figure it out by taking 9 from each side and multiplying it by four.*

From Sinead: *All you had to do was add the top and bottom which is 10 + 10 = 20 and then add the two sides 8 + 8 = 16 and then add them together 20 + 16 = 36.*

Quinn wrote: *take the bottom and the top and add them. then add the sides and theres your answer.*

$$
\begin{array}{r}
10 \\
10 \\
8 \\
+8 \\
\hline
36
\end{array}
$$

Aneitra wrote: *I think Jason had a good method because there are four sides and one of the sides has ten. You have to tell how many squares are around the border. So you multiply 10 × 4 and come up with 40. Then I subtract 4 because I have to take out a corner and come up with 36.*

From Steven: *The easiest way to find out the number of squares in the border is 9 × 4 = 36.*

Hasani wrote: *You can figure this out by multiplying 9 and 4 because it is easer then doing anything else.*

From Zack: *You can figure it out by 8 × 8 inside subtract 64 from 100 = 36.*

Jason wrote: *You add the squares on the border then subtract the 4 corners that you don't use.*

Jesse wrote: *You can figure this out by the Tami 9 on each side method. Each side has ten sqares but you can't count the corners twice. So you just multiply 9 × 4.*

From Rachel: *Take away the border and find how many squares are left 8 × 8 = 64 Then subtract 64 from 100 and you get the answer*

The border Problem
The border has 36 squares.

You can figure this out by multiplying 9 and 4 because it is easer the doing any thing else.

Algebra
Double stuff
'10
10
8
+8
36

take the bottom and the top and **add them**. then add the sides and theres your answer.

Students explained how they figured how many squares were in the border.

Jeremy wrote: *You can find this out by taking the number off the top which is 10. Then you add two sides which are 9 each and then add the bottom which is 8.*

$$\begin{array}{r} 8 \\ 9 \\ 9 \\ +10 \\ \hline 36 \end{array}$$

Juliette wrote: *You can figure this out by adding the 2 vertical sides and then adding the 2 middles which add up too 8 so 10 + 10 = 20 and 8 + 8 = 16 so 16 + 20 = 36*

I decided to focus the next lesson on helping the students improve their ability to explain their reasoning in writing.

Day 2

To prepare for this lesson, I wrote five of the explanations the students had written on large sheets of newsprint. I planned to use these examples to talk about what parts of the explanations were clear and what parts needed more information. Also, I planned to edit each of the explanations to model for the students how to make improvements.

I posted the chart of the six methods I had recorded the day before. Then I posted one of their explanations. I chose one of the more complete explanations to review first:

You can find this out by taking the number off the top which is 10. Then you add two sides which are 9 each and then add the bottom which is 8.

$$\begin{array}{r} 8 \\ 9 \\ 9 \\ +10 \\ \hline 36 \end{array}$$

"Which method does this explain?" I asked.

Several hands went up. "It's like number 2," Juliette said, "the one that Robert said."

"That's right," I answered, "and the explanation is fairly clear. There is some missing information, however. The explanation doesn't tell where the 9 and 8 come from. Let's start with the 9. Why are the two sides 9 each?"

"I can explain," Robert said. "It's because you already used the corner."

"That's just the kind of information that should be included," I responded, and inserted "because you can't count the corner again" into the explanation.

"How can you explain the 8?" I then asked.

I called on Michael. "You already counted both corners for the last row," he said, "so you can't count them."

I added "without the two corners" after the 8. The explanation now read:

You can find this out by taking the number off the top which is 10. Then you add two sides which are 9 each because you can't count the corner again and then add the bottom which is 8 (without the two corners).

$$
\begin{array}{r}
8 \\
9 \\
9 \\
+10 \\
\hline
36
\end{array}
$$

I added one more comment. "Including the numerical representation is a good idea," I said, "because it adds to the explanation."

I then went on to a second explanation, also a fairly complete one:

I think Jason had a good method because there are four sides and one of the sides has ten. You have to tell how many squares are around the border. So you multiply 10×4 and come up with 40. Then I subtract 4 because I have to take out a corner and come up with 36.

"I didn't write that," Jason called out.

"No, Aneitra did," I answered. "She was describing the method you explained."

"It seems clear to me," Zack said.

"I think so, too," I said, "except that I have two changes to recommend." I changed "one of the sides" to "each of the sides" and "a corner" to "all four corners." Though these were small changes, I wanted them to know that I expected careful reading and attention to all details.

I posted another:

You can figure this out by multiplying 9 and 4 because it is easier than doing anything else.

"There were more explanations of this method than any of the others," I said. "Though it was a popular choice, none of the explanations had enough information. What's missing is an explanation of why it makes sense to multiply 9 and 4."

"I can explain," Tami said. She came to the board and drew just the border of squares with 10 on a side.

"See," she continued, "you count 9 on each side by stopping before the last one so you don't count the corners twice." Tami illustrated this by counting and marking the squares she had drawn.

"Your explanation makes sense," I said. "How can I describe what you did in writing?"

Tami was stumped. Andy raised his hand. "You take a corner off each side," he said, "and that leaves 9."

"Then what?" I said.

"You do 9 times 4," Tami added.

I rewrote the explanation on the chart:

Take one corner off each side. That leaves 9 on each side. Then multiply 9 times 4 to find out how many squares in the border.

"This isn't the only possible way to explain Tami's method," I said. "There isn't one right way, but you have to be sure that what you write has all the information needed to make sense."

I then posted a fourth explanation:

Take away the border and find how many squares are left 8 × 8 = 64 Then subtract 64 from 100 and you get the answer

I went through a similar discussion, talking with the class about explaining why multiplying 8 times 8 made sense and where the number 100 came from. Also, I reminded them to include a period at the end of each sentence.

The last explanation I posted read:

take the bottom and the top and add them. then add the sides and theres your answer.

$$
\begin{array}{r}
10 \\
10 \\
8 \\
+8 \\
\hline
36
\end{array}
$$

First I corrected the grammar, adding capital letters at the beginning of each sentence and an apostrophe in *theres*.

"Having the numbers included helps," I said, "but I think the explanation would be clear if you explained why you added the two 8s."

"They're the sides," Tri said.

"Why does 8 make sense for the sides?" I asked.

"Because you can't count the corners again," Aneitra answered.

I edited the explanation to read:

Take the bottom and the top and add them. Then add the sides which are 2 less than the top because you can't count the corners again, and there's your answer.

"Now," I said to the students, "I'm going to post one more. This time, each of you is to write in your notebook an improved version of what I've posted." I posted an explanation that was another version of a method we had already discussed:

You add the squares on the border then subtract the 4 corners that you don't use.

The students' explanations showed improvement.

Krystal wrote: *There are ten squares on each side. You can't count any square twice. So subtract four corner squares. Now there are 36 squares.* Krystal included a diagram to illustrate her explanation.

Steven wrote: *OK you have 10 squares on each side and there are 4 sides so then you multiply 10 × 4 which is 40 but you have added the corners twice so you have to take out the 4 corners which makes it 36 squares. 10 × 4 − 4 = 36.*

From Juliette: *You add the top which is 10 and then the next side which is ten (counting the corner you've already counted). Add the bottom which is ten and then the next side up which is ten. And then you subtract the 4 corners that you counted twice each.* Juliette also included a numerical recording.

Zack wrote: *There are 10 squares on each side. Multiply 10 × 4, then subtract the corners (4), because you counted each twice.*

From Tami: *You count the 10 on each side and you get 40. Then subtract the 4 corners because you counted all corners twice and then you come up with the answer 36.*

The students' revised explanations showed improvement.

Hasani wrote: *You add the number on the top and then multiply it by 4 and then you subtract the corners that you used all ready.*

Andy wrote: *Assuming that the sides don't overlap on the corners, you multiply the 10 squares on a side by four for the four sides. Then you subtract the overlapping corners.*

The student who had the hardest time was Tri, a Vietnamese boy, who has lived in the United States for only three years and has difficulty with English. Tri wrote: *We count each side of borders are 10, we subtract 4 because we count twice on the corner.* Practice with writing is necessary for Tri to learn to express his ideas in more conventional English.

When I noticed that most of the students had written an explanation, I interrupted them to give additional directions. "I'm going to give each pair of you a worksheet I've prepared. When you complete your explanation," I said, "compare what you've written with your partner. Agree on one way to write this explanation and record this for number 1 on the worksheet. Then work together to write improved versions of the others on the worksheet."

I had included five explanations on the worksheet, all taken from what the students had written in their notebooks the day before. The students worked for the remaining twenty minutes rewriting the explanations on the worksheet.

When I read the worksheets that night, only one pair of students had completed all five explanations. I was faced with the natural difficulty that some students work more quickly than others. I wanted to give the others time to finish their work while keeping them all moving toward describing the methods algebraically. I decided to give an additional problem to extend their work into figuring out the borders of squares of different sizes.

Day 3

I began the class by drawing a 5-by-5 grid on the chalkboard. "How many around the border of this grid?" I asked.

I waited, giving the students a chance to think about the problem. When more than half the hands were raised, I called on Steven. "There are 16," he said.

"How did you figure that out?" I asked.

"I did it by Tami's method," he said. "I multiplied 4 times 4."

"Who did it a different way?" I asked. In this way, students again had the opportunity to describe the different methods for figuring the border.

"When you finish rewriting the explanations," I said, "then you are to find the number of squares in the border of grids of different sizes. Record your answers on a chart like this one." I drew a chart for them on the chalkboard, filling in the answers they already knew.

Number of squares on edge	Number of squares on border
3	
4	
5	16
6	
7	
8	
9	
10	36

"Underneath your chart," I said, "write what you notice about the pattern in the borders as the grids increase in size."

"Can we draw the squares to figure them out?" Andy asked.

"Yes," I answered, "making a drawing often helps in solving problems."

"Can we do this first before we finish the writing?" Joe asked.

"No," I answered, "you need to complete the other work and have me check it before you begin this."

There were no other questions, and the students got to work. Near the end of the period, all but two had finished what I had assigned. I asked those two to finish their work as homework. I called the class back to attention and told them that tomorrow we would be talking more about how algebra can be related to the border problem.

"Oooh, that's going to be hard," Sinead said.

"How many of you think algebra is going to be hard to learn?" I asked. Sinead and Joe raised their hands.

"I don't think it's going to be hard," Robert said, "but I don't think it's going to be easy." There was general agreement with Robert's feelings from the class.

"We'll see tomorrow," I said. I felt they were anxious but also interested and curious.

Day 4

I began the fourth day's lesson by discussing the charts on which the students had recorded the number of squares in the borders of grids of different sizes. They all had noticed that the number of squares in the borders increased by 4 as the number of squares on the edges increased by 1.

Number of squares on edge	Number of squares on border
3	8
4	12
5	16
6	20
7	24
8	28
9	32
10	36

"Why do you think this is so?" I asked.

"Because squares have four sides," Krystal said. Several of the others nodded in agreement.

"No, because they have four corners," Steven said. More nodded or murmured their agreement with Steven's thought.

"I think I know why," Zack said. Zack had come to be respected by the others for his understanding of math, and he had the attention of the class. "It's kind of like what Krystal said," he continued. "When the edge of the squares increases by 1, the border increases by 4 because 1 square is added to each side."

"That's it," Steven said.

"I don't get it," Rachel said.

"Look," Steven said, "every time a square is bigger by 1, you have to make each side bigger by 1, so that's like adding 4."

"Does anyone have another way to explain that to Rachel?" I asked.

"I can," Jesse said. "Adding 1 to each side is adding 4 altogether, and those 4 are on the border, so the border gets bigger by 4."

"Is there another way to say that?" I probed. There were no other volunteers. Rachel and the others seemed satisfied.

I was pleased that Zack offered his idea. I much prefer it when ideas such as these come from the students instead of from me. The class always seems to be more curious about and receptive to a class member's ideas than to mine. My ideas are taken more as pronouncements, laden with the authority of my position. (If Zack hadn't offered his idea, however, I would have offered an explanation. Then I would have asked for others to explain my idea in their own words.)

At this point, I moved ahead in my lesson plan. "Suppose I told you that I had a grid in my pocket," I said, "and that I wanted to figure out how many squares were in the border. Who could explain how to do it?"

About a third of the students raised their hands. I called on Halbert. "Go slowly, Halbert," I said, "because I'm going to write down what you would do as you explain it."

"First count the squares on an edge," he said. I stopped him so I could write this on the board. Then I asked him to continue.

"Multiply that number times 4," he continued, "and then subtract 4." I wrote that on the board as well.

Steven explains to Rachel why the number of squares in the border increases by four as the number of squares on the edges increases by one.

"Anything else?" I asked.

"No," Halbert said, "that tells you the answer." I wrote that as well. I had now written:

First count the squares on an edge. Multiply that number by 4 and then subtract 4. That tells how many squares are in the border.

"Do you agree that this method works for any size grid?" I asked. The students indicated their agreement.

"That makes it a method that is generalized," I said. "It works for all grids, not just the ones we've been exploring. Algebra is a way of describing a generalized method. Let me show you how I could translate Halbert's method to algebra."

"That wasn't Halbert's method," Jason blurted out. "That was my idea." Jason's need for attention was characteristic of him.

"Yes," I acknowledged, "Halbert described the method you first reported in a more generalized way." That seemed to satisfy Jason for the moment.

"Because I don't know yet how many squares are on the edge," I continued, "I'm going to use a letter instead of a number. I'll use e to represent the number of squares on the edge. What shall I use to represent the number of squares in the border?"

"B," several students called out together.

"So I'll write Halbert's generalization like this," I said, and wrote on the board:

$$e \times 4 - 4 = b$$

"This formula says that if I multiply the number of squares on the edge, e, by 4 and then subtract 4, I'll know how many squares are in the border. That's an algebraic way to express the method."

There were positive reactions to this. "That's cool." "I get it." "That's not so hard." "Yeah, that's OK."

Andy raised his hand. "I learned that you could write $4e$ instead of e times 4," he said. I wrote that on the board and explained to the class that this was OK, that when a number and letter were written together like this, it was understood that it meant to multiply.

"Could you write $e4$ instead?" Juliette asked.

"No," I answered, "the number is written first. Also, though it's not necessary, you could use parentheses as punctuation when you use the times sign." I wrote the first formula again with parentheses. Now there were three formulas on the board:

$$e \times 4 - 4 = b$$
$$4e - 4 = b$$
$$(e \times 4) - 4 = b$$

"Each of these three formulas," I said, "describes how to apply Jason's original method to a grid of any size. This formula doesn't describe the other methods. Tami, for example, didn't multiply the edge by 4 in her method. She removed one corner from each edge first before multiplying."

"How do you write that in algebra?" Hasani asked.

"I know," Jesse said. "You have to use e minus 1 instead of e." I wrote "$e - 1$" on the board.

"Can you explain why that makes sense to you?" I asked.

"Because you take 1 away from each edge, and that's e minus 1," Jesse said.

"I get it," Hasani said.

---

① $4e - 4 = b$

② $e + e - 1 + e + e - 2 = b$

③ $4(e - 1) = b$

④ $e + (e - 2) \times 2 = b$

⑤ $2e + e - 2 \times 2 = b$

⑥ $e - 2 \times 4 + 4 = b$

Border problem in Algebra

1. $(e \times 4) - 4 = b$
2. $e + e - 1 + e - 1 + e - 2 = b$
3. $(e - 1) \times 4 = b$
4. $(e \times e) - (e - 2)^2 = b$
5. $e \times 2 + e - 2 + e - 2 = b$
6. $e - 2 + e - 2 + e - 2 + e - 2 + 4 = b$

Working in pairs, students wrote formulas to describe each of the methods.

I continued with directions. "Working with your partner, try to write formulas for the other five methods," I said. "Though you'll work together, each of you should record in your own notebook. If you get stuck, try writing an explanation in words first and then translate it to a formula."

The students were willing to try this assignment. Their discussions were animated. Most found some way to write a formula for each method. The method that gave most of the students difficulty was Zack's method of removing the middle and leaving just the border.

I collected their notebooks at the end of class to see what they had accomplished. When I looked at their work, I found a great variety in what they had written. Some formulas were correct and others were incorrect.

As with any lesson, I now had a decision to make about what to do. It made no sense to belabor the work for those who understood. And it did not make sense to belabor the work for those who did not yet understand. My goal for this instruction was to give the students a beginning experience with algebra that I could build on over time. Though I would have liked each student to be able to write formulas easily and correctly, for the methods we had been studying, this wasn't the case. (It rarely is in a class.)

What I decided to do was to give the formulas some more attention for part of the next class, then have them write about their individual experiences with the lesson.

Day 5

I began class by writing on the board five different formulas the students had written for method number 5—adding the top and bottom edges and then the sides, each 2 less than the top and bottom.

$$e + e + e - 2 + e - 2 = b$$
$$e \times 2 + e - 2 + e - 2 = b$$
$$2e + (e - 2) \times 2 = b$$
$$e + e + (e - 2) + (e - 2) = b$$
$$e \times 2 + e - 2 \times 2 = b$$

"What's the same and what's different about each of these algebraic formulas?" I asked.

"They all explain Chris's method," Michael said.

"Some use times and some don't," Steven said.

"Some have parentheses and some don't," Andy said.

"What do the parentheses do?" I asked.

"They make it clearer," Juliette said.

"It looks neater," Jesse added.

"More than that," I said, "parentheses are sometimes necessary." I pointed out to the students that in the last formula I had written on the board, it wasn't clear that I was to multiply the quantity of e minus 2 by 2. I added parentheses. Then I asked them what else they noticed about the formulas.

"They all work," Zack said.

"With the parentheses added to the last formula, I agree with you," I said. "However, all the formulas you wrote did not work. I'm going to give you a chance to take another look at what you've done, this time with other students so you can get different points of view. I'm going to organize you into groups of three instead of partners so you have more formulas to compare."

I did this and had the groups work for about ten minutes. During this time, I talked with the groups that asked for help. There was much sharing of ideas and much erasing in notebooks.

When I interrupted them, I asked them to write a lesson log about this experience. Writing lesson logs is an idea I learned about in a workshop on writing in math and science I attended at the Lawrence Hall of Science in Berkeley, Calif. The workshop was given by teachers involved with the Bay Area Writing Project.

In my adaptation of the idea, I have students describe what has happened during the lesson and what they have learned so that it would be possible for someone who is not present to have a sense of what has occurred. I ask that they include as many details and specific examples as possible. I also require that their logs be about one page in length. The form I ask them to use is this:

Date of lesson:
General title: (Describing the lesson)
Description: (What went on)
Math content: (What you learned about)

This was the students' third experience writing a lesson log, and their approach to writing was more purposeful than in either of their earlier attempts. I circulated as students wrote. When someone asked me if what he or she had written was OK or enough, I had a stock answer. "That's a good beginning," I would say. Then I would add, "Include more examples," or "Explain more about what you learned," or "Write more about the mathematics."

As with all their writing, I gained insights into their thinking. Their comments about algebra revealed their perceptions and understanding.

Juliette wrote: *We learned about the beginning of algerbra and how to take a normal problem and change it to an algerbra equation.*

Chris wrote: *I learned about basic Algebra. How to make equastions and how to seperate algebraic promblems. I at first had a hard time figuring out what e & b ment but I figured out what they ment at the end. For example, e ment the question and b ment the answer.*

Hasani wrote: *Algebra is not easy but its not as hard as people say it is if you put your mind in.*

From Krystal: *I think algebra is finding new ways to write things and solve things, shortening things and extending things. I also think it helps you use your mind in difficult situations.*

From Jesse: *Algebra is a way of generalizing mathematics. You substitute letters for numbers. When we did it we used E for Edge and B for Border. This activity was just right because we had small groups.*

Michael wrote: *We learned about different ways to solve problems and there is no best way although one may fit you better than another. Some of us learned something about algebra.*

Jason wrote: *Algebra is the way to write how to figure out the problems. There are many ways to write algebra. Algebra is a way of adding, subtracting, dividing and multiplying letters to mean something with numbers.*

From Alesia: *I think algebra is letters that discribe numbers.*

Halbert wrote: *I think algebra is another way to find the answer to a math problem.*

MATH LESSON LOG

Date: Oct. 13, 14, 17, 18, 19

The Border problem

Description: First Mrs. Burns had us try to figure out all the different ways to find the border of a square that has 10 on each side. First thing that popped into everybody's head was 40 but you have to eliminate the corners which we already counted. The way I found the easiest was to count the 2 horizontal sides which are ten (with corners) and then count the two vertical sides which is 8 which you multiply by 2 and add to the 2 tens which add up to 20.

The next day we worked on improving the way that Mrs. Burns had written problems on a sheet of paper so they were easy to understand. Next we wrote all 6 of the ways to figure the border out into algebraic equations for algebra. Zach's was the hardest to figure out. His was to multiply the two edges (10x10, exe) and then that gives you the area of the whole square and then he took the area and subtracted just the middle which was everything but the border which turned out the equation was $exe - exe - 2 = b$. This unit helped us understand equations better. It helped us not just do the problem, but understand how we did the problem.

Math Content: We learned about the beginning of algebra and how to take a normal problem and change it to an algebra equation.

Logs help students reflect on their learning experiences and also help teachers assess students' understandings and misconceptions.

Math Lesson Log

October, 14, 17, 18, 19
ALGEBRA=
THE BORDER PROBLEM

Description: We try to find out the border of a square by counting the edge, add the four edges, and then subtract the four corners. Here is an example. We cut it down, shortened it into a different form.

$$e+e+e+e-4=b$$
$$(e \times 4) - 4 = b$$
$$4e - 4 = b$$

Math Content: I think algebra is finding new ways to write things and solve things, shortening things and extending things. I also think it helps you use your mind in difficult situations.

Math Lesson Log.

Date: October 13, 14, 17, 18, 19,
Title: Algebra:
The Border Problem.

Description: We have been working on the border problem for the past five days. We had a square and we tried to figure out the area of the square, when we found it it was 36. Then we had to figure out how someone got that.

Math Content: I learned about basic Algebra. How to make equations and how to seperate algebraic promblems. I at first had a hard time figuring out what e & b ment but I figured out what they ment at the end. For example e ment the question and b ment the aunser.

$$(e-1) + (e-1) + (e-1) + (e-1) = B$$

This equations means, edge-1 + edge-1 plus edge-1 plus edge-1, then B would be the final aunser.

Final Thoughts

Looking at the students' notebooks later, I noticed that although there was improvement in their formulas, there were still errors. Clearly, not all the students had "mastered" generalizing arithmetic procedures to algebraic representations. This did not concern me.

I've come to understand that partially grasped ideas and periods of confusion are natural to the learning process. I've come to understand that students' mathematical knowledge is developed, elaborated, deepened, and made more complete over time. I've come to understand that I cannot expect all students to get the same thing out of the same experience. (The *Mathematics Model Curriculum Guide, Kindergarten Through Grade Eight* from the California State Department of Education [1987] includes these notions as guiding principles for teaching for understanding.)

I feel that students benefited from the lesson in different ways. Zack, Jesse, Juliette, Krystal, and others gained insights and facility with algebraic notation. Sinead, Quinn, and Rachel learned that there was more than one way to solve a problem. Halbert and Joe learned more about the benefits of working collaboratively with others. Tri gained experience with expressing his ideas about math in English. Hasani learned he could do something he thought was hard.

And I learned more about each of my students, which will help me better meet their needs as the year progresses.

3

PATTERNS AND FUNCTIONS

California's *Mathematics Model Curriculum Guide, Kindergarten Through Grade Eight* (1987, 35) states the following:

> Looking for patterns helps bring order, cohesion, and predictability to seemingly unorganized situations. The recognition of patterns and functional relationships is a powerful problem-solving tool that enables one to simplify otherwise unmanageable tasks and to make generalizations beyond the information directly available.

This chapter presents activities that make ideas about patterns and functions accessible to students. Eight days of instruction with a class of seventh graders are described.

Students were first introduced to the idea of growth patterns and then used Color Tiles to create patterns of their own. Students analyzed other students' patterns and made predictions about how these patterns could or "should" grow. After an investigation of how increasingly larger squares grow, the students engaged in several investigations with cubes. In all activities, students were able to demonstrate and verify their thinking with the tiles and cubes. The materials were tools for making ideas about patterns more concrete.

Though students were introduced to writing formulas to express the generalizations of functional relationships, I kept the emphasis on their concrete explorations of building growth patterns and analyzing them geometrically and arithmetically.

Day 1

To prepare, I assembled eight plastic bags of Color Tiles with about 100 tiles in each. I had these on the counter ready to distribute to each group of four students.

"What comes to mind when I ask you to think about pattern?" I asked to begin the class. "Talk about your ideas in your groups and have one person record what you discuss." It was quiet for a moment before their discussions started.

After a few minutes, I called the groups back to attention. "Choose someone from your group to report one thing from your discussion," I said. I gave them a minute to do this.

Mark was first. "Our class schedule is a pattern," he said. "Like, it goes 1, 2, 3, 4, 5, 6, and the next day it goes 6, 1, 2, 3, 4, 5. We end today with fourth period, and we start tomorrow with fourth period." Our school is on a rotating schedule, so classes meet in a different time slot daily.

Teddy reported next. "The week is a pattern," he said, "Monday, Tuesday, Wednesday, Thursday, Friday, Saturday, Sunday."

Pam reported for her group. "There are patterns in clothes," she explained, "like when you have stripes, like on my shirt."

"How many of you have patterns in the clothing you're wearing today?" I asked. Students looked around at what everybody was wearing. Quite a few raised their hands.

Sheila then reported for her group. "Wallpaper has patterns," she said.

"Piano keys have a pattern," Aurora said, "like white, then black, white, then black."

"Daily life has a pattern," Richard said. "You go home, cool off, eat, play, do homework, eat dinner, watch TV, brush your teeth, and go to bed. It's a rotating order."

"All the patterns you reported," I said, "are examples of things that repeat over and over. The pattern makes it possible to predict what will come next."

"Is that what patterns are?" Tami asked, "things that repeat?"

"Things that repeat are one kind of pattern," I answered. "Once you understand a repeating pattern, you can tell about what comes next. For example, even though wallpaper stops at the end of the wall, you can describe what would come next in the design. It's predictable."

I was interested, however, in focusing the students on patterns that grow rather than patterns that repeat. Since none of their examples described growth patterns, I introduced this idea with two examples.

"Mathematicians rely on patterns to make predictions in many sorts of problems. I've planned a collection of activities to help you learn how mathematicians use patterns to make predictions. In these activities, however, the patterns aren't ones that repeat. Instead, they're patterns that grow."

"Like how?" Nguyen asked.

"Here's an example," I said. "There's an old favorite math story about a boy who agreed to wash the dishes every night to earn some money. He said he'd charge just a penny."

"No way," James said.

"That was just the first night," I continued. "He said he'd charge $.02 the second night, then $.04 the third night, then $.08, and so on. Each night he doubled his fee."

"Oh, yeah," Natalie called out. "I heard that story. He makes a lot of money, like millions or more in a month."

"That's impossible," Paul said.

"Let's figure it out," Mark said.

"How would you figure it out?" I asked.

"It's easy," Mark answered. "You just keep doubling."

"That's an example of a pattern that grows instead of repeats. He doesn't earn the same thing over and over, but you can predict what he'll earn the next night because of the pattern of doubling."

"Can we figure it out?" Aurora asked.

I hadn't planned to take class time to have them do this, but because their interest was high, it seemed best to let them satisfy part of their curiosity.

"Figure out how much he would be paid on the tenth night of washing dishes," I said. "Check with others in your group to see if you agree."

After a few moments, the students had come to consensus that he would be paid $5.12 on the tenth night.

"Not bad for washing dishes," Greg said.

"But it's not millions," Paul said.

"I noticed that most of you listed each day's salary to figure out how much he earned on the tenth day," I said. "You know the pattern, so you can keep going. But I don't want you to do more figuring now. Right now I want to focus on helping you understand more about how mathematicians use growth patterns."

I waited until I had everyone's attention.

"Here's another example of a pattern that grows," I said.

I showed them an article titled "Faces from the Future" that appeared in the February 13, 1989 issue of *Newsweek* magazine (Cowley and Springer 1989, 62). There were three pictures with the article: a photograph of an eight-year-old girl, a computer-generated portrait of the same girl as she might look as a fourteen-year-old, and an actual photograph of her taken at age fourteen. The computer picture was generated from the photograph of the girl as an eight-year-old. It had been used successfully to find the girl six years after she had been abducted by her father. The similarity between the computer portrait and the actual photograph is impressive.

I reported to the class from the article. "The article explains that changes in 39 facial measurements were used by the computer," I said. "The measurements included the length of the nose, the width of the mouth, and the space between the eyes. The article says, 'The seeming magic all stems from the fact that facial bones change in predictable ways throughout childhood.' For example, the article explains, 'the distance from the bridge of the nose to the base of the chin typically increases 12 percent between the ages of 6 and 13.'" The students were intrigued by this information. Some made comments. "That's neat." "Can I see those pictures?" "How do they do that?" "They're really close."

"In this situation," I told the class, "being able to make predictions about patterns of growth helped solve a kidnapping case. Making predictions from growth patterns is an important area of mathematics that we'll be studying for a while. For the rest of class today, you're going to experiment with growth patterns using Color Tiles."

In the past, I've begun instruction about patterns by giving students patterns to investigate. However, I've come to learn that when students understand the purpose of what they're being asked to learn, they are more motivated. Also, an introduction such as this can add to students' understanding of the role of mathematics in our society.

I then drew a sequence of four squares of increasing size on the overhead.

"Why do you think I would call this sequence of squares a growth pattern?" I asked the class.

"Because they're getting bigger," Tina said.

"They're like just enlargements," Russell said.

"Suppose I want to draw the next square in the sequence," I said. "What would I draw? Talk in your groups about this. Then I'll have someone give me directions to draw the square that comes next."

I gave them a few moments to talk together. After hands were raised by all but two groups, I called on Kimberly.

"It would be a square that has five small squares across the top and bottom and down the sides," she said.

I drew a five-by-five square on the overhead. "Yes, this is the fifth square in this pattern," I said. "I could continue the pattern by drawing increasingly larger squares. This is an example of a growth pattern that's fairly obvious."

I then drew a small square on the overhead. "I'm going to start another pattern the same way I started the square pattern," I said. The next idea is an adaptation from an activity in *Unit I: Seeing Mathematical Relationships* (Bennett, Maier, and Nelson 1988), the first of six units in the Math and the Mind's Eye materials.

"This is the first in the pattern. When I add squares to make it grow to the second in the pattern, I get this." I drew an L-shaped pattern using three squares.

"It may not be as obvious as it was with the squares what the next pile would look like," I said. "As a matter of fact, there are several different ways to continue the pattern of growth, so my next question doesn't have just one right answer. What might the next pile look like?" Several students raised their hands immediately, but I didn't call on any of them.

"I don't want to hear your ideas yet," I said. "Instead, you each are to use one color of tiles and build the two figures I've drawn on the overhead. In a moment, one person will get a plastic bag of tiles for your group. When you've built what I've drawn, think about how these might grow into the next pile and use more tiles of the same color to build what you think the third pile might look like. Then, using the same pattern of growth, build the fourth pile and cover it up with a sheet of paper. While you're working, be thinking about how you can explain how your piles grew."

I gave one more direction. "Before you get started building your individual patterns," I said, "talk in your groups to make sure everyone understands what to do." I had given a hefty amount of information, and I know that some students have difficulty following verbal directions. I felt that having them talk among themselves would help orient all of them to the task.

After a few minutes, I called the class to attention. "Share your growth pattern with the other members of your group," I said. "See if you can predict each other's fourth piles."

Some groups had two or three different patterns. In some, everyone had the same pattern—the L. There were some students in the class who had no idea how to make third or fourth piles.

Students use tiles to show how the pattern might grow.

After the groups had had time to look at the patterns group members had made, I interrupted them. "Who can describe a third pile for me to draw?" I asked.

Denise volunteered. "I built a pile with a row of three going up and down, and right next to it a row of two going up and down." Denise's group confirmed that I drew it correctly.

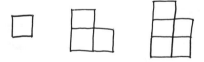

"How did Denise add tiles to the second pile to make it grow?" I asked.

"She added one on the top left and one on the top right," Kimberly answered.

Greg had a different idea. "I thought she added two on the bottom," he said.

"Either way seems to produce the same result," I said. "There often are different ways of looking at the same thing. How might you describe what this third pile looks like?"

"It looks like a building with a chimney," Norberto said.

"It's like a building with a room knocked off," Teddy said.

"Now build what you think the fourth pile in Denise's pattern would be," I then said.

The students did this quickly. I drew on the overhead what I saw on the desks and Denise's group confirmed it was correct.

"Suppose we continued this pattern," I said. "Can you predict what the twentieth one in the pattern would look like? Close your eyes for a moment and try to imagine its shape. Raise your hand when you think you can see it."

I purposely didn't ask how many tiles would be used for the twentieth pile or how tall it would be. I wanted them to focus on the idea of growth geometrically. I've found that focusing on number often moves the investigation from looking at growth patterns to getting the right numerical answer. There would be time later for numerical interpretations.

I waited until more than half the class had raised their hands. I then called on several to describe what they had envisioned.

"It's more like a tall skyscraper with two columns," Tami said.

"It's a high building with a short chimney," Paul said.

"It's still a building with a room knocked off," Teddy said.

"Did any groups build a third pile that's different from the one Denise described?" I then asked. Several students raised their hands. It was just about the end of the period.

"I'm interested in your other patterns. We'll start tomorrow with this again," I said. "It's time to put away the tiles. Also, it may be a good idea for someone in your group to make a sketch of your third and fourth piles if they're different from what Denise described." There was the usual bustle of getting ready to leave.

Day 2

I drew the first four piles in Denise's pattern on the overhead as a reminder of what we had been doing yesterday. Also, I distributed the Color Tiles.

Underneath Denise's pattern, I drew the first two piles again so that other third and fourth piles could be added and compared with what Denise had built.

"Who can come up and draw a third pile that's different from what your group discussed yesterday?" I asked.

Richard came up and drew an L shape.

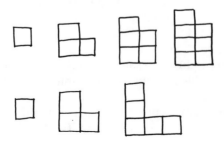

"That's like ours," Conroe said.

"Ours, too," Kimberly said.

"Quickly take out some tiles and build what the fourth pile will look like," I said. Everyone in the class was able to build the next in the pattern.

After the students had time to build the fourth pile, I drew it on the overhead.

"How does this pattern grow?" I asked.

"You just add one to each end," Pam said.

"You get a bigger L each time," Conroe said.

"There are two lines with an overlapping corner," Patty said.

"Show me with your hands," I said, "what the twentieth pile will look like." Some held their arms out to make an L. Others used just their hands. Some sketched an L in the air.

"Does any group have another growth pattern?" I asked. I drew the first two piles again. Teddy raised his hand and came up to draw another third pile.

"Now build what the fourth one will look like," I said to the class. They did this fairly quickly. Their confidence seemed to be increasing.

"Who can describe how you built the fourth pile?" I asked.

Ron raised his hand. "I saw a slanted row of two added to the first pile, and a slanted row of three added to the second pile, so I added a slanted row of four to the next pile." I drew the fourth pile, adding slanted rows as Ron described.

Richard described a different way. "I built a vertical row of four, then of three, then of two, then one," he said.

Pam saw it differently. "I just added another row on the bottom that had one more in it," she said.

"What would the twentieth look like?" I asked. Hands shot up.

"A big staircase," Aurora said.

"A long, jagged edge, like teeth," Conroe said.

I then introduced an activity for them to do in pairs. "Now you'll have the chance to build growth patterns that you invent. You'll work in pairs, with the person seated next to you. Together, build four piles in a growth pattern using Color Tiles."

"Do we start with one tile like you did?" Tami asked.

"You can," I answered, "but you don't have to."

Some students began to get to work. I interrupted them to give further directions.

"Record your work so others can look at the first three in your pattern, then predict the fourth," I said.

Tami raised her hand. She had an idea about how to record. "If we fold the paper into four columns," she said, "then you can fold one flap over and hide the fourth drawing underneath." Tami showed the class what she meant.

Her suggestion made good sense. "Let's do it that way," I said. "When you're done, you'll have the chance to trade papers and see if you can figure out others' growth patterns."

The class got right to work. I helped those who had difficulty getting started. The students were all involved and seemed interested. A few partners finished in time to trade papers. Most completed the assignment, but a few needed a bit more time. I collected their papers at the end of the period.

That night, I examined their work and sorted their papers into three groups. There were seven that were complete and had predictable growth patterns. There was one that was complete but had an error in the fourth drawing. Five weren't finished. I decided to structure the next day's lesson so that I could work with students who needed help while the rest examined the patterns made by other groups.

Day 3

I began the period by explaining how the students were to analyze others' patterns. "Use a half sheet of paper for each pattern you analyze," I began, "and write your names and the names of the people who created the pattern. Then look at their first three drawings and together predict what the fourth drawing would look like. Use the tiles to build it or make a sketch. Then check to see what they drew.

"After you check your prediction, describe how the pattern grows. Finally, draw what you think the fifth pile will look like."

"What about if we didn't finish our own patterns yet?" Norberto asked.

"I've separated the unfinished papers, and I'll pass those back first," I said. "Then I'll give the rest of you someone else's pattern to analyze."

I then handled some of the management details. "We'll keep the papers organized in three piles up here at the front of the room. The first pile is for finished patterns ready to be analyzed by others. The second pile has half sheets of paper for you to use. The third pile is for your completed analyses."

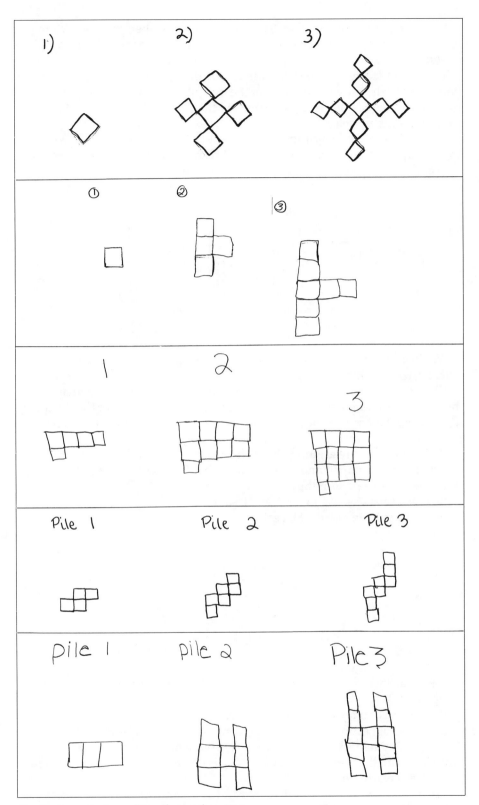

Students created a variety of growth patterns.

I circulated through the room distributing the unfinished papers. "When you finish," I said, "put your paper on pile 1 and take someone else's pattern to analyze."

Then I randomly distributed patterns for the others to analyze. "I've prepared three extra growth patterns for the first pile," I said. "That way, we won't run out if some of you work more quickly than others." I distributed forms to these students as well.

Finally, I returned Jessica and Roger's pattern to them to talk about why their fourth pattern didn't make sense to me. I showed them their first three drawings and asked them to explain their growth pattern.

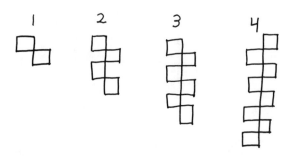

"We just added 2 more each time like this," Jessica said, pointing to 2 squares with corners touching.

"How can you explain your fourth drawing?" I asked. They immediately saw the error they had made. Instead of adding 2 more to an end of the third pile, they had split them and added a tile to each end. They saw how to correct their paper and got to work.

Mark and Hal were arguing about their unfinished work. There were three drawings on their paper, and they needed to add the fourth. I asked them to describe the growth pattern they were trying to show.

"It doesn't make sense to me," Mark said.

"He didn't like my idea," Hal said.

"What was your idea?" I asked.

"Well, I thought we'd add some on the side and then some on the top and bottom," he said, showing me the first three drawings.

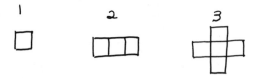

"But you have to do the same thing," Mark said. "You can't just keep changing."

"But I wanted to make it harder," Hal said.

"I have a suggestion," I said. "Hal, continue with your idea and draw the fourth pile. Then Mark, see if you can figure out what Hal is thinking and make a fifth pile with the tiles. What Hal is doing is complicated, but I think it is predictable and reasonable."

I then talked with Brett and Richard. They had a pattern for which the number of tiles they used grew predictably. They explained to me that they had used 1, 3, 5, and then 7 tiles.

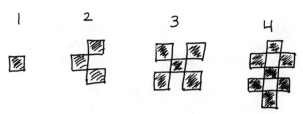

"I see that," I said, "but I don't see any orderly way the arrangements of the tiles are growing. I can't predict what the next will look like." The boys decided to abandon their plan and start again.

As with most assignments, there was a range of responses. For some students, the assignment was easy, and they whipped through analyzing several patterns. When I checked what was being put in the pile of completed work, however, I returned several for more explicit explanations. For others, the assignment wasn't as simple, but it was appropriate. There were a few students for whom the idea of growth pattern still didn't make sense.

I gave the class the homework assignment of analyzing a pattern I had created. I drew the first four in my pattern and had them copy my sketches. "For homework," I said, "analyze my pattern as you've been analyzing each other's. Tomorrow you'll begin class by comparing your work."

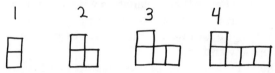

That night, I reviewed their analyses of their classmates' patterns. Students took different approaches when describing them. Some focused on the patterns visually and described their shapes.

They're like stairs with more and more steps each time.

It would always have a line of squares with one sticking out.

They have four branches and every other one the branches are the same and then the other one two branches are different.

Other students did not describe the shape of the patterns but gave numerical analyses.

You just double the number for each one.

They added two tiles in each pattern so you go plus two each time.

Some students' descriptions included both geometric and arithmetic analyses.

The two rows keep going up vertically. They added one to each row each time.

It's always an odd number in a row plus one sticking out.

After looking at and thinking about their work, I decided to focus on encouraging all students to look at patterns both geometrically and arithmetically.

Day 4

While the groups compared their homework at the beginning of class, I checked that individuals had done the assignment. The homework had been easy for the students.

I then gave them an additional challenge. "Discuss in your groups what the twentieth pile would look like and how many tiles I'd need to build it," I said.

I could tell that this also was easy for the class. There was some quick discussion and then around a dozen students raised their hands. I called on Paul.

"There would be a row of 20 tiles with one on the top on the left, so it would have 21 tiles," he said. There were nods of agreement.

"What about the hundredth pile?" I asked. Lots of hands went up. I called on Brett.

"There would be 101," he said, "a row of 100 and one extra."

"What about the thousandth pile?" I asked. Again, there were lots of hands. Natalie explained that there would be 1001 tiles.

"What about if I wanted to know how many tiles I needed for the forty-third or hundred thirty-seventh, or any other pile?" I asked. This also was obvious for them.

"You just add one," Richard said, "because you'll always have a long row with one on top."

"Here's how mathematicians might describe my pattern," I said. I wrote "$n + 1 = t$" on the overhead.

"You take the number of the pile," I said, pointing to the n in the equation, "and add one on top and that gives you the number of tiles." I pointed to the t.

I've learned from past experience that representing growth patterns algebraically moves the investigation into an abstract realm that is often out of the students' experience. Though I wanted to introduce the idea that a formula can describe a growth pattern, I gave this explanation with a light touch. It seemed to make sense to them, but I didn't emphasize it or push it any further. My goal wasn't to get them to write formulas; rather, it was to focus them on investigating patterns numerically and spatially.

"Let's try another," I said. "Here's a growth pattern we talked about the day before yesterday." I drew it on the overhead.

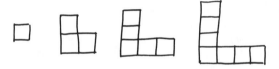

"Oh yeah, the L," Conroe said.

"Talk in your groups about how many tiles would be needed to build the twentieth L," I said.

This wasn't quite as obvious as the homework pattern, but after a few minutes about half a dozen hands were raised. I gave the groups a few more minutes to work and then brought the class to attention. I called on Kimberly.

"We figured 39," she said. There was a chorus of agreement.

"Explain how you got it," I said.

"Well, it's 20 up and then 20 across," she said, "but you can't count the corner twice, so you subtract 1."

"You did the number of the pile plus the number of the pile and then subtracted 1," I said. I wrote "$n + n - 1 = t$" on the overhead. Again, I treated the formula incidentally, as a way to record what Kimberly had reported.

Richard's hand shot up. "We did it another way," he said. "We didn't count the corner, so there were 19 on the two pieces. Then we added the corner last."

Aurora had another way. "We just added 20 for the vertical," she said, "and then 19 for the flat side."

"Hearing your different methods is a good reminder that there's more than one way to look at a problem," I said. "You should always look for another approach even when you think you've found the answer."

I then drew on the overhead the other two patterns we had investigated the day before yesterday.

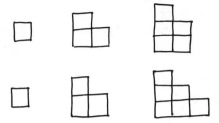

I had the students work in their groups to consider the twentieth pile of each. "Decide how the twentieth pile will look and how many tiles are needed," I said.

I circulated as the groups worked. They were focused and their discussions were animated.

Pedro came up to me. "Look," he reported, "the towers are just like the L's except the short side is up instead of flat." He was pleased with his discovery.

I interrupted the class when all groups had figured how many tiles were needed for the first pattern and most had completed the second as well. About ten minutes remained in the period.

I sketched the four drawings from Pam's and Greg's pattern on the overhead. A few of the students in the class recognized it as one they had analyzed the day before.

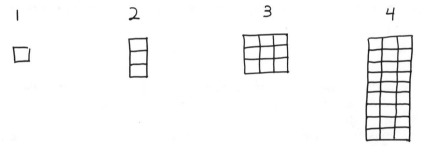

"Discuss this growth pattern in your group," I said. "Don't figure how many are in the twentieth pile. Just discuss how it's growing." There was an immediate buzz in the class that died down in a moment. Five hands were raised. I called on Huy.

"It just goes times by 3," he said.

"That's what we got," Aurora added. "1, 3, 9, 27."

I called on Natalie next. "The next one would be a square, because it goes square, column, square, column," she said. Others nodded.

"What would be the dimensions of the square in the next pile?" I asked.

There was some discussion among groups. Several hands were raised. I called on Rodney.

"It would be 9 by 9," he said.

"How do you know?" I asked.

"I don't know," he said at first. I waited a moment. Rodney then added, "Well, the first square was 1 by 1, and the second one, you multiplied by 3 to get 3 by 3, so I just multiplied by 3 again."

"What do you think about Rodney's prediction?" I asked Pam and Greg. They smiled and nodded.

"What about the twentieth in their pattern?" I then asked. "Decide in your group whether it would be a square or a column and why."

The group discussions were animated. I brought them back to attention after several hands were raised. I called on Jaimi.

"It would be a column," she said, "because the odd numbers are all squares and the even numbers are all columns." Again, there were nods of agreement.

I then gave a homework assignment. "You're to investigate your own growth patterns for homework," I said. I projected the directions for the assignment on the overhead:

Homework

1. What would your 20th pile look like? Describe in words.

2. How many tiles would you need to build your 20th pile? Explain how you know.

"As you're copying down these questions, I'll distribute the patterns you and your partner made for others to analyze," I said. "Each of you needs to make a sketch of your four drawings because I'm going to collect these patterns before you leave class. With the remaining time in class, talk with your partner about the problem. Tomorrow you'll compare your answers and reasons." They spent the rest of the time getting their homework assignment organized.

Day 5

To begin class, I had pairs compare their homework as I circulated to check that they had done the work. I noticed that though a few students had difficulty with the assignment, most were able to describe how their twentieth pile would look and how many tiles were needed. Most had included diagrams in their descriptions.

Roger wrote the following for his and Jessica's pattern: *The 20th one would have 20 tiles down the left and 20 tiles down the right. It would have 40 tiles because you just double it like number 1 had two tiles.*

Hal used a sketch to describe the twentieth one in his and Mark's pattern. He wrote: *The 20th one will look like this. It will have 39 tiles. I will have 9 tiles going up from the center tile and 9 going down from the center tile. And there will be 10 to the left from the center and ten to the right.*

Kelly and Cheryl had built a staircase pattern. Kelly wrote: *There would be 20 vertical rows, with 39 blocks on the far right column. Each row descends to the left, subtracting 2 blocks each column and centering the columns until there is 1 block left in the middle. It would have 400 blocks. I know this because I added the number 2 less than the present one until I got to 1. That equaled 400.*

My initial plan was to have pairs generalize and describe a method for figuring the number of tiles in any pile. I had even hoped to encourage them to write formulas. However, I decided to scratch this plan. I realized that most of their growth patterns were much more complicated than the $n + 1$ or $n + n - 1$ examples I had given. Also, they seemed to have spent enough time on their

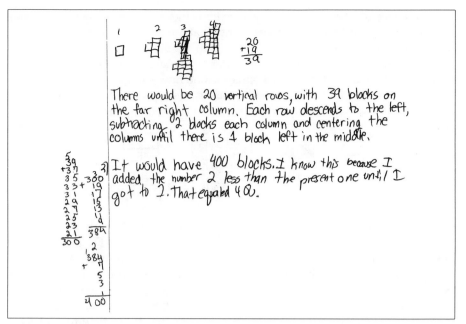

There would be 20 vertical rows, with 39 blocks on the far right column. Each row descends to the left, subtracting 2 blocks each column and centering the columns until there is 1 block left in the middle.

It would have 400 blocks. I know this because I added the number 2 less than the present one until I got to 2. That equaled 400.

$$
\begin{array}{l}
39 \\
+37 \\
\hline
35 \\
33 \\
31 \\
29 \\
27 \\
25 \\
23 \\
21 \\
\hline
300
\end{array}
\qquad
\begin{array}{l}
3 \\
380 \\
+19 \\
17 \\
15 \\
13 \\
11 \\
\hline
384
\end{array}
$$

$$
\begin{array}{l}
384 \\
+ \quad 7 \\
\quad 5 \\
\quad 3 \\
\hline
400
\end{array}
$$

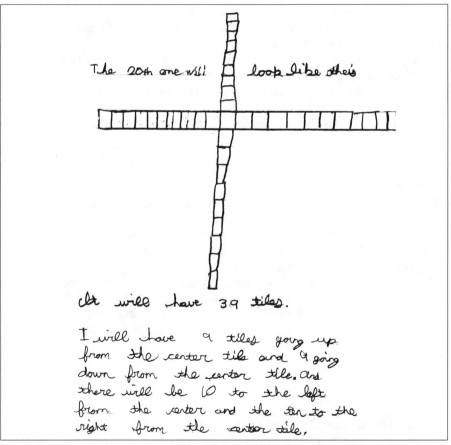

The 20th one will look like this

It will have 39 tiles.

I will have 9 tiles going up from the center tile and 9 going down from the center tile. And there will be 10 to the left from the center and the ten to the right from the center tile.

For homework, students described what their 20th pile would look like and how many tiles they would need to build it.

own patterns, so I decided to return to an investigation of the growth of squares and move them into several investigations about the growth of cubes. I collected their homework and called the class to attention.

"A few days ago, we looked at the pattern of squares," I began. "I want to return to this familiar pattern and again examine how squares grow."

I used overhead tiles to build four squares, using colors to accentuate how many were added to each square to get the next larger square.

I introduced the class to the story interpretation of growing squares presented in *Mouse and Elephant: Measuring Growth* (Shroyer and Fitzgerald 1986), one of the books in the Middle Grades Mathematics Project materials.

"Imagine that the smallest square is a square on its first birthday. It's a one-year-old square. The next one is a two-year-old square on its second birthday, and so on. Focus on how many tiles are added each year," I said, "and discuss in your groups how the squares grow." After giving them time to do this, I asked what they had noticed. Lots of hands went up.

"I'm interested in hearing all your ideas," I said. "Also, I want you to listen carefully to what others have to say."

"They grow in an L shape," Pam said. "You have to add a bigger L each time." Many nodded.

Brett reported next. "You go up by 2s," he said. I didn't understand what Brett meant. Richard interpreted for him.

"He means you add 2 more each time. Add 3, then add 5, then 7, and so on." Again, many nodded.

"How many tiles would be added to get from the nineteen-year-old square to the twenty-year-old square?" I asked. "Talk about this in your groups. You may need to use paper and pencil."

In a few minutes, I asked the class to come back to attention and called on Steven.

"It would be 39," he said. "We made a chart all the way to 20, and it came out to be 39." The class agreed that 39 was correct.

"Did anyone figure it a different way?" I asked.

Aurora hesitatingly raised her hand and tried to explain her complicated process. "Well, for the two-year-old," she said, "you added 3, and 3 is one more than 2, so 3 plus 2 equals 5 for the next one." I couldn't follow her reasoning. No one else could either. Aurora came up to the overhead and wrote the following:

3 years: $3 - 1 = 2$
$3 + 2 = 5$
4 years: $4 - 1 = 3$
$4 + 3 = 7$

She explained again. "You subtract 1 from the pile number and add that answer to the pile number and you get the number of tiles to add for the next square. So 20 would be 20 minus 1 equals 19 and 19 plus 20 equals 39."

Still, not too many others understood her reasoning. Jaimi, however, raised her hand. "Mine is almost the same as Aurora's, but not quite," she said. "Take any year. Take the year before it and add the two together. That will give you the number of tiles to add. For 20, you add 19 and 20, which is 39."

I then focused them on figuring the total number of squares. "You have different ideas for how many tiles to add each time," I said. "Now I'd like to have you look at the total number of tiles for each square. Do this for squares from one year old to ten years old."

Some students starting writing on scratch paper. Some began to discuss in their groups. Others stared at the screen with thoughtful expressions. I had thought describing how squares grow would be immediately obvious to them, but it wasn't. After a few minutes, I called the class to attention. Kelly explained what she had discovered.

"I found a pattern," she said, "and I can tell how many tiles no matter how old the square is. For 1, it's 1; 2 is 4; 3 is 9." I recorded as she reported. "1 times 1 is 1," she elaborated. "2 times 2 is 4, 3 times 3 is 9, and so on. So for the ten-year-old, it would be 100 because 10 times 10 is 100." About half the class nodded. No one had a different way to report.

I then gave the students an assignment to do individually. "Describe all you can about how squares grow," I said. "Show your data, include drawings, and give convincing arguments for what you write." The class settled into work.

Greg drew eight squares of increasing sizes. He wrote: *It gets gradually bigger and it is amazing how fast it grows. Look how big the 8 is compared to 1. 1 × 1 = 1, 2 × 2 = 4, 3 × 3 = 9, etc. Multiply the age by itself and that gets the answer.*

Conroe wrote: *You always add 1 more than the # of squares. Example . . . if the age is 2 then there is 4 squares, so you just add 5 to get age 3. Another way is you just multiply the age by itself. Example . . . if the age is 6 then you multiply 6 by 6 which is 36. That is how to find the # of squares.*

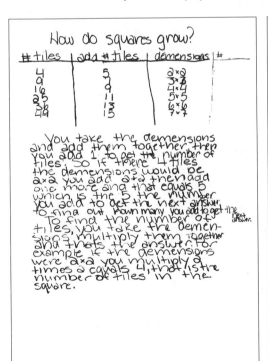

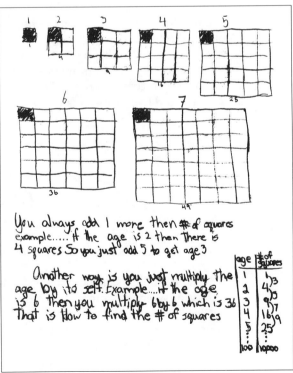

Students were asked to describe all they could about how squares grow.

Kimberly wrote: *You take the dimensions and add them together, then you add 1 to get the number of tiles to add to get the next answer. So if there are 4 tiles you add 2 and 2 and then one more and that equals 5 which you add to 4 to get the next answer. Or you take the dimensions and multiply them together. For example, you 2 times 2 equals 4. That is the number of tiles in the square.*

At the end of class, I told them that tomorrow we'd investigate how cubes grow.

Day 6

To prepare for the next day, I assembled a small plastic bag for each group with about 100 two-centimeter interlocking cubes, the kind that can be snapped together to make three-dimensional shapes. Also, I listed these terms on an overhead transparency:

faces

edges

vertices

To begin, I left the plastic bags on the counter and gave each group just 1 cube. I held up a large cube for the class and asked, "Can anyone explain what *faces* or *edges* or *vertices* of a cube are?"

The only word they knew for sure was *vertices*. (We had studied angles earlier in the year.) I told them what faces and edges were.

"Discuss in your groups how many faces, edges, and vertices a cube has," I said. All of the groups counted 6 faces and 8 vertices correctly, but more than half of them counted only 8 of the cube's 12 edges. I've found this to be a common mistake.

I then held up one of the two-centimeter cubes. "This is the size of a one-year-old cube," I said. "Have one person get a bag of cubes for your group and then build what you think is a two-year-old cube."

They got involved enthusiastically. There were three different solutions. Three groups correctly built a 2-by-2-by-2 cube. Two groups snapped together 4 cubes, and two groups used only 2 cubes.

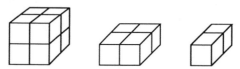

I called the class to attention and held up the large cube and a box of tissues. "Both of these have 6 faces, 8 vertices, and 12 edges," I said, "but the box of tissues isn't a cube. What makes a cube a cube?"

Steven raised his hand. "They're all squares," he said. "I mean, every side is a square."

"Why isn't the tissue box a cube?" I asked.

Rena answered. "Some of the sides are rectangles," she said.

"Yes," I said, "in a cube, all the faces are squares." I modeled the correct terminology. "Some of the structures you built to represent a two-year-old cube aren't cubes. Try again."

After a moment, all of the groups had correctly built a 2-by-2-by-2 cube. I then explained the investigation I wanted the students to try.

"As a group," I said, "build a two-year-old, a three-year-old, and a four-year-old cube. For each, answer two questions. How many one-year-old cubes does it take to build it? And how many cubes are there that aren't visible from the outside?" I wrote the questions on the overhead.

"I don't get it," Mark said.

"With a two-year-old cube," I explained, "you can see all 8 cubes you used to build it. But with larger cubes, some will be inside."

"I know," Elizabeth called out, "there's one inside the three-year-old cube." She already had assembled a three-year-old cube, and she showed it to the class. The class was intrigued. The idea of cubes not being visible seemed to spark their curiosity.

"After you've investigated the two-year-old, three-year-old, and four-year-old cubes," I said, "look for patterns and see what you can predict for larger cubes."

I circulated and watched the groups work for about fifteen minutes. Jaimi's group was upset with her. As the recorder, she was writing numbers without consulting the others. I saw that all her predictions were wrong for the cubes that weren't visible. I talked with the group about the importance of using the materials to verify their ideas and the importance of the recorder's recording only what the entire group agreed on. They worked more effectively after that.

In another group, Rodney and Sharlene, who were both usually reluctant math students, got very interested. They were systematic and helpful in their group's investigation.

David had built a four-year-old cube with a two-year-old cube inside that could be removed. Pam's group had made a hollow six-year-old cube. I gathered some of the students to show how cubes of some sizes fit inside others. This sparked a new direction in the class, and other groups began to experiment.

Cheryl, Rena, Natalie, and Huy came up with a generalization. They wrote: *In a 4 year old cube you can fit a 2 year old cube inside, in a 5 year old cube you can fit a 3 year so you minus 2 to get the one you can fit into.*

Aurora, Tiambe, and Elizabeth came to a similar conclusion. They wrote: *To get the no. of cubes not visible you minus 2 from the age then figure out the no. of 1-year old cubes in that age.*

Three other groups had figured out how many invisible cubes there were for three-year-old, four-year-old, and five-year-old cubes but hadn't related the numbers to dimensions of cubes and didn't come to generalizations. Two groups were working more slowly and were concentrating on the number of cubes needed to build each one. I encouraged them to think about the invisible cubes as well.

Rodney came up to me with a two-, three-, four-, and five-year-old cube, one stacked on top of the other. "It's just like the squares," he said excitedly. "There's an L around them."

It was now near the end of class, so I had them get organized and ready to leave. "Don't break apart your cubes," I said. "Put them in the bags intact and put in a slip of paper with your group's names on it. You'll continue tomorrow." I collected their work. It had been an exciting class.

Rodney stacked two, three, four, and five-year-old cubes to show his discovery about how they grow.

Days 7 and 8

I began class by reading aloud the generalization that Cheryl, Rena, Natalie, and Huy had written. "Discuss in your groups why this is true," I said to the class. "Use the cubes to prove it. If you're stuck, raise your hand, and Cheryl, Rena, Natalie, or Huy will come and help." I knew that not every student was going to grasp this generalization now. Some would need more experience before they would be able to understand it. But I wanted to begin class by getting them back into thinking about the cube patterns they had been investigating.

I also directed a comment at the group that had written the statement. "Talk about how you could convince someone that what you wrote is true," I said.

I read the statement once more and let the groups discuss it for a few minutes. I then called the class back to attention and introduced another investigation about cubes.

"Today you'll begin to explore a problem about painted cubes," I said. I held up a 2-by-2-by-2 cube.

"Imagine that I dip this cube in a bucket of paint," I said, "a bucket of magic paint that dries instantly. Then I remove the cube from the bucket and break it apart into one-year-old cubes. How much of each one-year-old cube is painted?"

> 3 year old = 27 one year old cubes
> 2 years old = 8 one year old cubes
> 4 years old = 64 one year old cubes
>
> * In the three year old cube there is 1 cube
>   you can not see.
>   In the four year old cube there are 8 cubes
>   you can't see.
>
> * It takes 15,625 cubes to make a 25 year
>   old cube.
>
> In a 4 year old cube you can fit
> a 2 year old cube inside, in a 5 year
> old cube you can fit a 3 year so
> you minus 2 to get the one you
> can fit into.

Cheryl, Rena, Natalie, and Huy wrote about their investigation of cubes that grow.

Most of the students immediately saw that three faces of each cube would have paint on them. Richard explained.

"Each cube was on a corner," he said, "and three sides were showing." This seemed obvious to many of the students.

"OK," I continued, "suppose I did the same with a 3-by-3-by-3 cube. How much of each cube would have paint on it? Talk about this in your groups."

The groups all scrambled for three-year-old cubes. Their discussions were animated. I overheard a variety of comments.

"Look, there's one inside that doesn't get painted at all."

"The corner ones all have three sides painted."

"How many corners are there?"

"The rest only get painted on one face."

"No, here's one that would get two faces painted."

"Is there only one without paint?"

"There's nine on each face, so I think you do 6 times 9."

I called them back to attention and asked what they had discovered. They reported the kinds of statements I had overheard.

"Were there any cubes with more than three faces painted?" I asked. Several students answered no.

"Could there be if the cube were larger?" I asked. "Talk about this in your groups."

In a moment, I called them back to attention and called on Pam. "The ones in the corners get the most paint," she said, "and they only have three sides showing. There's no way to get more painted."

"So you found cubes with three, two, one, and zero painted faces," I said. There were nods.

I drew a chart on the overhead projector and had the students help me fill it in:

Age	0 faces	1 face	2 faces	3 faces
2-yr-old	0	0	0	8
3-yr-old	1	6	12	8

I then described the investigation I wanted the students to do. "In your groups, investigate what happens to larger cubes when they're dipped in the bucket of magic paint. Make a chart like the one I've shown and continue recording. Look for patterns."

"How high do we go?" Pedro asked.

"I suggest you do at least four-year-old and five-year-old cubes," I answered. "Then see if you have enough information to predict what would happen for a six-year-old cube. Write statements about any patterns you find."

The students were eager to get started. They worked for the rest of the period and continued the next day. Interest stayed high. As I circulated, I encouraged students to write generalizations about what they noticed.

Aurora wrote the following for her group: *To predict how many are hidden minus 2 from the age and bring that number to the 3rd power. To get how many have 1 face painted subtract 2 from the age and multiply that no. by itself then the answer by 6. To get the no. of how may cubes have 2 faces painted subtract 2 from the age then multiply that no. by 12. All cubes have 8 separate cubes with 3 faces painted.*

Richard wrote for his group: *3 faces painted is always 8 because there are 8 corners. The cubes that are needed is age³. 2 faces painted is always age minus 2 × 12 because on one edge there is 2 less than the age because you don't count the corners and there is 12 edges. 1 face is always age minus 2 × age minus 2 × 6 like the one above because its a square then times 6 because there is 6 faces. 0 faces is the number of cubes needed of a cube with a two age difference.*

I had these two groups compare their statements to decide whether they had come to the same conclusions.

Tami's group came up with different sorts of statements. They looked at the patterns of numbers in the charts but not at how they were generated. They wrote: *For cubes needed the last number goes in a pattern odd, even, odd, even, odd, even. For 1 face painted they are multiples of six. For 2 faces painted just add 12. For 3 faces painted they are all even numbers.*

Groups that finished early compared their statements. For homework, I asked students to write what they knew about cubes. Mark asked how much they needed to write.

"About one page," I answered.

Reading students' writing gives me information about what they experienced and helps me be more sensitive to individuals' needs. Most students revealed that they had a basic sense of what cubes were.

Age	0 faces	1	2	3
3 year old	1	6	12	8
4 year old	8	24	24	8
5 year old	27	54	36	8
6 year old	64	96	48	8
7 year old	125	150	60	8
10 year old	216	384	96	8

Prediction Pattern

To predict how many are hidden minus 2 from the age and bring that number to the 3rd power. To get how many have 1 face painted subtract 2 from the age and multiply that no. by 2 then the answer by 6. To get the no. of how many cubes have 2 faces painted subtract 2 from the age then multiply that no. by 12. To get how many cubes

All cubes have 8 separate cubes with 3 faces painted.

3 faces painted is always 8 because there are 8 corners.

The cubes that are needed is age³ because l×w×h = volume.

2 faces painted is always age-2×12 because on one edge there is 2 less than the age because you don't count the corners and there is 12 edges.

1 faces is always age-2 like the one above (no corner) × 2 because its a square then times 6 because there is 6 sides faces

0 faces is the number of cubes needed of a cube with a two age difference. The big one covers it.

Working in groups of four, students presented their work about the painted faces of cubes.

Elizabeth's paper was typical of many students' papers. She listed what she knew:

Cubes have eight corners always.

Cubes have six sides always.

Cubes have twelve edges.

Cubes can be made into bigger cubes.

A ten-year old cube has 1,000 cubes in it.

When building cubes to figure out how many have two faces painted you just add twelve starting with a two year old cube and zero cubes with two faces painted.

Some students wrote paragraphs. Often, they provided information that hadn't been included in these activities. Pam, for example, wrote: *I know that every cube has to have six even faces, and eight vertices. They also have to have twelve edges. I know that a cube is not a square because a square is two demensional and a cube is three demensional, also a square has area and a cube has volume. I know that if you throw a cube up in the air it has a 16½% chance that one face will show up.*

Art expressed his lack of success and confidence. He wrote: *Well, I've been struggling with this particular subject. I know they have 6 faces, 8 corners, and 12 edges, and all that but I just have a lot of trouble. I was thinking about coming after school for help. I'm sorry I can't tell you more. I know more things about it but I don't know how to put them in words.*

I had students share what they wrote with the others in their groups. I talked with Art and the other students who had said they were having trouble. Though we took a break from focusing on patterns after these experiences, the thinking permeated all that we did afterward. Students naturally looked for patterns in whatever math they were exploring. That was a worthwhile payoff.

Final Thoughts

Teaching five classes a day makes it hard to get to know students in great depth. It's especially hard when I teach from the front of the room and only hear from those confident enough to offer their thoughts in a class discussion. However, in lessons such as described in this chapter, when students are actively investigating problems, working with concrete materials, and interacting with one another, I have more opportunity to observe them and learn about their thinking processes. Also, the students are more invested in their own learning. They're involved, they communicate their thoughts, and they seem to enjoy math class. Though getting organized for these classes was demanding, the results justified the effort.

PROBABILITY INVESTIGATIONS

Probability is often overlooked as a topic in the middle-school math curriculum. This is unfortunate, as probability is an important area of mathematics that can motivate students' interest, stimulate their mathematical thinking, and reinforce their application of number skills.

Even when middle-school students have not been formally introduced to probability in school, they have some notion of what probability is about. Their notions usually have an intuitive base, however, and do not extend to any mathematically symbolic interpretation. This chapter presents classroom activities for introducing basic ideas, vocabulary, and notation of probability.

The lessons were taught to seventh and eighth graders. The students are shown how to use fractions to assign probabilities. They learn about randomness and what *fair* and *unfair* mean when applied to a game situation. And they engage in a sampling experiment that involves them with interpreting data and making inferences about the population of Color Tiles in a bag.

The first day's lesson is adapted from *Probability* (Phillips et al. 1986), one of the five books in the Middle Grades Mathematics Project materials. This valuable resource for teaching math to middle-school students is rich with ideas.

Day 1

"What does the word *probability* mean?" I asked the class to begin the lesson. Students had various ideas.

"It has to do with chances," Jesse said.

"Like if you toss a coin, it comes up heads 50 percent of the time," Hal offered.

"It has to do with odds," Sasha said.

"It tells you about something that may happen but may not happen," Robbie said.

"What situations can you think of that use probability?" I then asked.

"The lottery," several students answered in unison. This was an exciting time in the California lottery. Over $60 million had just been won. The students began to talk all at once about what they knew about the lottery. "You have to pick the six numbers." "Yeah, but you get to pick seven." "There's a 1 in a million chance." "No, it's 1 chance in 14,000." "That can't be." "I wish I could get lucky." "I know someone who won $100 once." "Hey, Ms. Burns, do you play the lottery?"

I settled the class down and asked if they could think of other situations in which probability is used.

"In weather forecasts," Joe said.

"In sports, too," Jay said.

"In games like with dice," Rachel said.

"In Las Vegas," Jason added.

I then turned their attention to an activity. I put 1 blue tile and 1 yellow tile in a paper bag. "If I ask one of you to draw a tile without looking," I asked, "what color will you draw?"

There was an outbreak of comments. "It would be blue." "No, yellow." "I say blue." "It better be yellow." "You can't tell." "I can tell. I say it will be blue." "No, you can't tell because it's 50-50." "Yeah, that's right, it's 50-50."

I called them back to order. I phrased the question differently. "If I asked a mathematician to answer the question about what color you would draw," I said, "what answer do you think I would get?"

This was not the first time the students were asked to think about drawing tiles from a bag, and their responses reflected their previous experience.

"A mathematician would say you couldn't tell because it's a 50-50 chance," Andy answered.

"That's what I said," Jason claimed, affecting an exasperated tone.

"Any other ideas?" I asked. Alison raised her hand.

"You could say that it's an equal chance to get either," she said.

"That's the same thing," Steven said.

"But it's expressed differently," I responded. "I'm interested in the different ways you express ideas. Can anyone think of another way to answer the question?" I think it's important, even if I get a correct response to a question, to ask for additional ideas. That way, students learn that there is more than one way to explain a thought or answer a question.

"There's a 50 percent chance of getting blue or yellow," Tami said. No one else volunteered another idea.

"Another thing a mathematician might say," I added, "is that you can't tell because the chance of drawing a blue tile is 1 out of 2, and the chance of drawing a yellow is 1 out of 2. Who can explain why that makes sense?"

About half the hands shot up. "Because there are two tiles in the bag," Julia said, "and one of them is blue and one is yellow."

I then showed how to represent the probability of an event as a fraction. I wrote on the chalkboard:

$$P(B) = \frac{1}{2}$$
$$P(Y) = \frac{1}{2}$$

"Who can explain what I wrote?" I asked.

Again, about half the hands were raised. I called on Michael. "It says that the probability of getting a blue is ½, and the same thing for yellow."

"Let's try it," I said. "You'll take turns drawing out a tile. We'll note its color, and then you'll replace it."

The first three students drew yellow tiles. There were cheers and groans.

"Before drawing again," I asked, "what would you predict about the next color to come up?"

"You can't tell," Steven said, "because it's a 50-50 chance."

"But it seems like you should get a blue one soon," Alison added.

"But you still can't tell," Jesse said.

"Is it possible that we could take 10 more draws and still not get a blue one?" I asked.

"I don't think so," Hal answered.

"It could happen," Tami said, "but it probably won't."

"It should come up 5 blues and 5 yellows," Andy added.

"But it could come up all yellows," Jesse insisted. "It is possible."

"So what do the mathematical probabilities tell you?" I asked.

"It gives you some idea of what might happen," Robbie said.

I then added a blue tile to the bag so that there were 2 blues and 1 yellow. "What is the probability of drawing a blue tile now?" I asked. I called on Julia.

"It's 2 out of 3," she said, "because 2 of the tiles are blue." I wrote on the board:

$$P(B) = \tfrac{2}{3}$$

"What's the probability of drawing a yellow?" I asked. I called on Steven.

"It's 1 out of 3," he answered. I wrote

$$P(Y) = \tfrac{1}{3}$$

Then I removed the yellow tile. "Now what's the probability of drawing a blue tile?" I asked.

"2 out of 2," Hal answered. I wrote

$$P(B) = \tfrac{2}{2}, \text{ or } 1$$

"When the probability is one," I explained, "then you know for sure it will happen. The chance is certain."

I then posed another question. "What's the probability of drawing a yellow tile?" I asked. Some students guffawed in response.

"It's zero," Jay said. I wrote:

$$P(Y) = \tfrac{0}{2}, \text{ or } 0$$

"If the probability of an event is zero," I said, "then the chance that it will happen is impossible."

I continued with other arrangements of blocks. I emptied the bag and put in 1 red, 1 blue, and 1 yellow. I first asked the students for the probabilities of drawing a red, then a blue, and then a yellow. I added one more of each color so that there were 6 in the bag. The students seemed to understand that this didn't change the probabilities.

I emptied the bag again and this time put in a different arrangement of 6 tiles: 3 blue tiles, 2 red tiles, and 1 yellow. We discussed the probabilities, and I recorded them on the board:

$$P(B) = \tfrac{3}{6}, \text{ or } \tfrac{1}{2}$$
$$P(R) = \tfrac{2}{6}, \text{ or } \tfrac{1}{3}$$
$$P(Y) = \tfrac{1}{6}$$

"What could you add to the bag so that the probability of yellow would change from ⅙ to ½?" I asked. This was more difficult for them. Several students made guesses, and I recorded each on the board.

Andy said, "Put in 2 yellows and take out the reds. Then you'd have 3 blues and 3 yellows."

"That works," I said, "but try and find a way to do it by just adding tiles without removing any."

"I know," Hal said, "add 3 yellows. No, add 4."

"What would be in the bag then?" I asked.

"You'd have 5 yellow and 3 blue and 2 red," he answered, "and that would work."

Jay raised his head from the writing he was doing on his paper and said, "You could add 1 blue, 1 red, and 6 yellow, and it would still work because then you'd have 7 yellow and 7 of the others."

"Is that right?" Steven asked me.

I recorded Jay's suggestion. Jesse and Tami verified for the class why it worked.

This part of the lesson had taken about twenty minutes. I continued with the next activity suggested in the resource book.

"Let's look at another probability situation," I said. "This is a game that's like a lottery. I'm going to assign each of you a number." There were 23 students in class. I wrote their names on the board in two columns of 10 each and one column of 3. I wrote a number next to each name, starting with 10 and ending with 32.

"Why can't we pick our own numbers?" Sasha asked.

"Aren't you going to give yourself a number too?" Quinn asked.

I ignored Sasha's question and answered Quinn's question. "Sure, I'll take a number," I said, writing 33 and adding my name.

Then I described the game. "I have two bags," I said. "In one bag, I've put 3 tiles. I've written the number 1 on one tile, the number 2 on another, and the number 3 on the third." I removed the tiles and showed them to the class.

"In the other bag," I continued, "I've put 10 tiles, and numbered them from zero to 9." I showed these to the class as well.

"In this make-believe lottery," I said, "a tile gets drawn from each bag. The number that is drawn from the first bag gives the tens digit of the winning number; the number from the second gives the ones digit. If a number comes up that I haven't assigned, such as 36, for example, then we put the 6 back and keep drawing another units digit until we get a winner."

I asked for a volunteer to put check marks next to the winning numbers. I chose Alison. Then I walked around the class and had different students draw from the bags. Excitement erupted. There was groaning, whining, cheering, and general rooting for numbers. Though noisy, it was in good spirits. I continued for 15 numbers, then quieted them down.

"Is this a fair game?" I asked. I elaborated by explaining what I meant by *fair game*.

"Asking you if the game is fair," I continued, "is the same as asking you if each person has an equal chance of winning. Does each number have an equal chance of coming up?"

This question resulted in an animated and wonderful discussion. About half the students contributed ideas, but everyone was attentive. Several students

Alison put check marks next to the winning numbers.

held to their initial ideas while others changed their minds during the discussion. Some students wavered back and forth in their thoughts.

I did not contribute ideas to the discussion. I quieted the class when too many students spoke at once. I reminded them several times to listen to each other. I responded to ideas by asking for other explanations. The arguments got more and more passionate, and finally consensus was reached. The game wasn't fair, and the people in the 30s had the advantage.

"How could the game be changed so it would be fair?" I asked. There were several suggestions.

"Get more people so there are more 30s," Joe said.

"Just list the rest of the 30s," Jay said, "and give those numbers checks if they come up but no one wins."

"Give the 30s less money," Andy said.

There were now about ten minutes left to the period. I asked the students to write in their notebooks. Having them write at the end of class gives them a chance to reflect on what occurred during the period and gives me insights into their perceptions. I asked that they write what they knew about probability.

That night I read what the students had written in their notebooks. Their thoughts revealed a range of understandings and misunderstandings. I do not correct students' ideas or give writing of this sort a grade; rather, I use it as a way to assess their mathematical progress and as a guide to making choices about what to include in subsequent periods.

Steven, for example, wrote: *Probability is a chance that can be taken in games or in real life like fliping a coin you have a fifty fifty percent chance of getting either heads or tails.*

Rachel wrote: *I know that probability has to do with chance.*

Alison wrote: *I now know how to find probability. All you do is take the number that you want to find out the probability over the number of all the tiles. You will then get a fraction which will then be your probability of the odds of doing something or of winning.*

From Jesse: *Probability is the chance of winning a game. Think about a coin toss, the probability of getting tails is 50% or ½. Probability is used in casinos and betting houses to figure out the odds of wining so they don't lose money.*

From Sasha: *I do not know very much about probability but I do know that it is the chances of something.*

Michael wrote: *I used to know a lot about probability but since I never use it I forget very easily. In the seventh grade I could do almost every probability problem anyone gave me but now I can only do easy things like if there are 3 cubes 1 red 1 yellow 1 blue what is the probability of picking a red = ⅓. Probobility is the mathematical form of predicting odds and chances.*

Joe wrote: *I don't know that much about probability but I am hopeing that you will teach us alot. I know that you use percents and fractions. Probability is what is probable of happening.*

From Andy: *Probability is often paired with statistics. It is the chances that something will happen. Hal gave a good example: If you flip a coin, the probability that it will come out a certain way is ½ or 50%.*

Robbie wrote: *Probability is the odds that something will happen again like winning the lotery and if you do winning it again.*

From Chris: *I just know that probability is when you find the probability of things.*

Jason wrote: *Probability is a guess that something will happen or come up. The lottery is a probability game.*

From Hal: *Probability is a way to find the ways to get how many time you get something. for example what is the probability of throwing up a coin and getting head or tails. it is 50%*

Julia wrote: *Probability is the odds of getting something or not getting something. Such as Hal mentioned, a coin has two sides it would be a 50/50 chance of either getting heads or tails.*

Day 2

To prepare for this day's lesson, I filled three bags with different assortments of red and blue Color Tiles. I wrote the three populations I used on the chalkboard:

A: 8 blue, 16 red

B: 16 blue, 8 red

C: 4 blue, 20 red

"I've written on the board the Color Tiles I put in each of these bags," I said, showing the class the three bags. "What I didn't do, however, is label the bags. So we don't know which bag has which population of Color Tiles."

The students were attentive and seemed curious. I continued with additional information. "In a few moments, I'll have someone choose one of the bags," I said. "Our class task will be to try and figure out which population of tiles is in the bag without looking inside, but instead by using some mathematical ideas of probability."

"Do you know which bag is which?" Robbie asked.

"No, I don't," I answered. "We'll all learn together if we predict correctly by checking the contents." None of the other students had questions at this time.

"Pick one of the bags, Alisa," I then said. I chose Alisa because she was sitting within easy reach of the three bags.

"In this experiment," I continued, "you'll take turns reaching into the bag without looking, drawing out 1 tile, and noting its color. Then you'll replace the tile, and someone else will have a turn."

"Why don't you just keep the tile out?" Jay asked. "Then we'll be able to tell what's in the bag."

"One of my purposes for this lesson," I said, "is to help you learn more about the mathematics of probability. I agree it would be easier to find out what is in the bag by taking the tiles out one by one. We could also just dump out the contents all at once and count the tiles. Instead, I'm interested in an experiment with the mathematical idea of making a prediction from a representative sample."

"Let's get on with it," Jeff said, impatient as always.

I wrote the numerals from 1 to 6 in a column on the board. "We'll need to keep track of the color of each sample draw," I said. Julia raised her hand and volunteered to record.

I started around the class, having six students in turn draw a tile and replace it. I shook the sack after each tile had been replaced. Julia recorded what was drawn.

1 B
2 R
3 B
4 B
5 R
6 R

"How do you know they're not picking out the same tiles each time?" Jason asked.

"Because she shook the bag each time," Alisa said.

"But the same ones could stay on the top," Jason pursued.

"But I didn't take mine from the top," Sasha said. "I reached into the bottom."

I interjected a question to redirect their thinking. "What fraction of our sample is blue?" I asked.

"One-half," Jay blurted out quickly, without waiting to be called on.

"Explain how you figured that," I said. I always have students explain the answers they give. I want students to learn that their reasoning is important, not just their answers. Also, too often, students are used to having their responses questioned only when they are incorrect. I want to keep the focus at all times in math class on the students' reasoning.

"We did 6 draws," Jay explained, "and 3 of them were blue. That's ½."

By calling out, Jay had prevented me from providing ample time for the others to think about my question. To avoid this, I included an additional direction when I asked the class my next question.

"What does the information from our sample tell you about what's in the bag," I asked. "Raise your hand if you have an idea about that." In this way, I reminded the class of the classroom procedure, making eye contact with Jay to let him know indirectly that I didn't want him to answer until recognized. Sometimes, discipline in this subtle way avoids confrontation and doesn't interrupt the learning activity.

About a third of the class had their hands raised. As some students talked, others put their hands down, feeling their ideas had already been expressed.

"It doesn't help at all," Andy said. "None of the possibilities you wrote on the board have half blue."

"But I know it can't be C," Alisa said, "because that only has 4 blue out of 24."

"You don't know for sure," Jason said. "They could have been picking the same blue one." Jason was still not convinced about the draws being random.

"I think it's A," Jeff said.

"Why?" Robbie asked. Jeff just shrugged.

"You can't tell yet," Alison said.

"Let's take 6 more samples and then see what evolves," I said. "Mathematicians would agree with Alison. There really is insufficient information to make a reliable prediction about the population in the bag." I wasn't sure that all the students were familiar with the words *insufficient*, *prediction*, and *population*. By using them in the context of their activity, however, I think students have the best chance to learn them.

I wrote the numerals from 7 to 12 on the board. I continued around the class having students make draws. Julia again recorded.

1 B	7 R
2 R	8 B
3 B	9 R
4 B	10 R
5 R	11 R
6 R	12 R

"What do you notice now?" I asked.

Hal raised his hand. "Lots more reds came up," he said. "It came up 5 times."

"That's weird," Sasha said.

"What's weird about it?" I asked.

"Why should so many reds come up now when they didn't last time?" she asked.

"It's not so many," Jay said. "5 is not so many more than 3."

"But it seems like lots more," Sasha added.

"What fraction of our 12 samples is blue?" I asked. "Talk about this in your groups and raise your hands when you agree on an answer and also can explain why you think it's right."

Having students discuss in small groups gives more of them a chance to verbalize their ideas. Also, talking in their groups gives students who are reticent to risk answering in front of the entire class a safer setting for voicing their thoughts. After a few moments, most hands were raised. I called on Sara.

"It's ⅓ blue," she said.

"Explain how you got that," I prompted.

"Because 4 of them were blue," Sara explained, "and there are 12 altogether, and that's $\frac{4}{12}$, and that reduces to $\frac{1}{3}$." Though most of the others nodded their agreement, I can't say for sure all the students really understood Sara's explanation. However, I knew I'd be asking for the same kind of reasoning again in the lesson and those who weren't yet secure with this idea would have more chances to think about it.

I then wrote on the chalkboard:

After 6 samples, $\frac{1}{2}$ blue

After 12 samples, $\frac{4}{12}$, or $\frac{1}{3}$, blue

"Let's compare what we know about our samples with the populations of tiles I wrote on the board," I said. "In your groups, figure out what fraction of each of the three populations—A, B, and C—is made up of blue tiles."

Not only did this give the students another chance to talk with each other about fractions, it also gave me the chance to circulate, listen, and learn more about how individuals were thinking. A common error in their group discussions was for students to compare the number of blue tiles and red tiles rather than the number of blue tiles and the total number of tiles. I overheard one group argue whether A had $\frac{1}{2}$ blue (8 out of 16) or $\frac{1}{3}$ blue (8 out of 24). All these discrepancies were resolved in the small groups' discussions.

As before, when I had students report what fractional part of each population was blue, I had them explain their reasoning. I wrote the fractions on the board.

A: 8 blue, 16 red $\frac{8}{24}$, or $\frac{1}{3}$, blue

B: 16 blue, 8 red $\frac{16}{24}$, or $\frac{2}{3}$, blue

C: 4 blue, 20 red $\frac{4}{24}$, or $\frac{1}{6}$, blue

Rachel's hand shot up. "Look," she said, "our fraction is the same as the A fraction." Though Rachel's language was imprecise, we all knew she was referring to the fraction of blue tiles in our 12 samples.

"See, I was right," Jeff said.

"Do we know for sure that we have population A?" I asked.

"We don't know for sure," Hal said, "but it's the best bet."

"It could be something else," Gretchen said. "You can't tell for sure."

"I don't really see how you can tell what's in the bag just from drawing tiles out like we're doing," Jay said. I used Jay's comment to give the class some information about sampling and probability.

"Let me tell you what mathematicians think about sampling," I began. "When you reach into the bag and draw out 1 tile, you're picking a tile at random." I wrote the word *random* on the chalkboard under the heading "probability and sampling."

"It's random because you can't predict what will come up on any single draw," I continued. "However, mathematicians have experimented and found that when you make many, many random draws, a pattern emerges. Probability is a way to predict that long-range pattern."

I then returned to the activity. "Let's continue taking samples to see what pattern emerges and see if more information makes you more secure about predicting what's in the bag," I said.

Students took turns drawing a tile from the bag.

I wrote the numerals from 13 to 18 on the board. Julia returned to her post for recording and I had six more students make draws.

1 B	7 R	13 B
2 R	8 B	14 B
3 B	9 R	15 R
4 B	10 R	16 R
5 R	11 R	17 R
6 R	12 R	18 B

Again, I had the students discuss in their groups what fraction of our 18 samples was blue. They all came up with the same answer. I added this information to the chalkboard.

After 6 samples, ½ blue

After 12 samples, $\frac{4}{12}$, or ⅓, blue

After 18 samples, $\frac{7}{18}$ blue

"Is $\frac{7}{18}$ more or less than ⅓?" I asked. "Discuss this in your group and raise your hand when you agree on an answer and can explain it." Some groups talked about this; some used paper and pencil to figure. When all but one of the groups was ready, I called on Andy.

"It's more," he said, "because if you wanted to reduce ⁷⁄₁₈ to thirds, you have to divide the top and bottom by 6, and 6 goes into 7 once with some left over, so it is a little more than 1."

"Does anyone have a different way to explain it?" I asked.

I called on Jennifer. "It's kind of the same," she said, "but I started with the ⅓ and made it into ⁶⁄₁₈, and that's less that ⁷⁄₁₈."

"Any other explanations?" I asked. I called on Matt.

"It's still closest to A," he said.

"Let's add 6 more samples and see what happens," I said, adding the numerals from 19 to 24 to the chalkboard. "Remember, we're looking for a convincing pattern in our results."

Again, Julia recorded. This time, all red tiles were drawn.

1 B	7 R	13 B	19 R
2 R	8 B	14 B	20 R
3 B	9 R	15 R	21 R
4 B	10 R	16 R	22 R
5 R	11 R	17 R	23 R
6 R	12 R	18 B	24 R

"Uh oh," Sasha said, "it's moving closer to C now."

"What's moving closer to C?" I asked.

"What we've been taking out of the bag," she answered.

"What fraction of our 24 samples is blue now?" I asked. Sara answered that it was ⁷⁄₂₄. I added this information to the board.

After 6 samples, ½ blue

After 12 samples, ⁴⁄₁₂, or ⅓, blue

After 18 samples, ⁷⁄₁₈ blue

After 24 samples, ⁷⁄₂₄ blue

"How does ⁷⁄₂₄ compare to ⅓?" I asked. "Figure this out in your groups."

It seemed immediately obvious to a few of the students that ⁷⁄₂₄ was smaller than ⅓. Others needed to use paper and pencil to compare them.

"Sometimes a picture can help reveal a pattern," I said. "See if this makes sense." I drew a graph of what had happened, explaining what I was doing as I drew it.

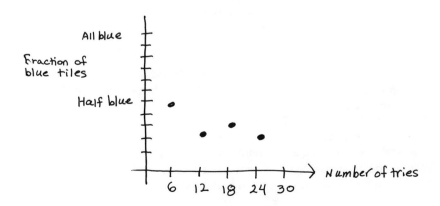

"Who can explain what this graph tells?" I asked.

Robbie raised his hand. "It shows that first we had ½ blue," he said, "but then we got closer to ⅓ blue, and the pattern looks like we have the A bag." Robbie and some of the others seemed to be able to interpret what I had drawn, but I wasn't sure all the students could do so. Still, I felt my making the drawing modeled for them another tool for understanding a mathematical pattern. We then continued with another set of 6 draws.

1 B	7 R	13 B	19 R	25 R
2 R	8 B	14 B	20 R	26 R
3 B	9 R	15 R	21 R	27 R
4 B	10 R	16 R	22 R	28 R
5 R	11 R	17 R	23 R	29 B
6 R	12 R	18 B	24 R	30 B

I added the fraction of blue tiles for the 30 samples to what I had already written on the board.

After 6 samples, ½ blue

After 12 samples, ⁴⁄₁₂, or ⅓, blue

After 18 samples, ⁷⁄₁₈ blue

After 24 samples, ⁷⁄₂₄ blue

After 30 samples, ⁹⁄₃₀ blue

"What do I do with my picture?" I asked. "Is ⁹⁄₃₀ more or less than ⁷⁄₂₄?"

This question resulted in an interesting discussion that revealed more about the students' understandings.

"You can't compare them because 24 doesn't go into 30," Jeff said.

"You can reduce ⁹⁄₃₀ to ³⁄₁₀," Julia said, "but that doesn't help."

"You need to make both bottoms the same," Jay said.

"I know," Alison said excitedly. "You can make them both sixths because 4 goes into 24 six times and 5 goes into 30 six times." I wrote on the board:

$$\frac{7}{24} = \frac{?}{6} \qquad \frac{9}{30} = \frac{?}{6}$$

"You have to divide the top and bottom by the same number," Jason added. Several of the students got out their calculators. I asked them to work in their groups to come up with answers.

"Can you write a decimal on the top of a fraction?" Robbie asked.

"Yes," I said.

"It looks weird," he responded.

I recorded what the students had figured:

$$\frac{7}{24} = \frac{1.75}{6} \qquad \frac{9}{30} = \frac{1.8}{6}$$

"So ⁹⁄₃₀ is bigger than ⁷⁄₂₄?" Tanya asked tentatively.

Sasha answered, "Yes, because 1.8 is like 1.80 and that's more than 1.75."

"They're almost the same," Josh added, "but 1.8 is a little bigger."

"So where do I draw the next dot on the graph?" I asked.

"Up a little," Gretchen said.

"Are you convinced about what is in the bag?" I asked.

There was a resounding agreement that it had to be A.

"Will you be disappointed if it's not A?" I asked.

"Not disappointed," Jeff said, "just surprised."

I emptied out the bag. Robbie and Jay counted 8 blue and 16 red.

I gave the students homework related to the class investigation. They were to respond to the following problem:

> There were some tiles in a bag. Students took turns drawing out a tile, noting its color, and replacing it. After 12 draws, they had drawn 6 red, 4 blue, and 2 yellow. Write what you know *for sure* about what is in the bag and what you know is *probably true*.

Processing Homework

I began class the next day by having the students discuss their homework assignment in small groups. "Compare what you wrote," I said. "To start, each of you should read what you wrote. Then discuss your ideas and try and come to agreement as a group about what you know for sure and what is probably true. While you're discussing, I'll come around and check that you've completed the assignment."

I find that having students discuss their homework in small groups gives them the chance to rethink their work. Also, students who didn't do the assignment, either because they were absent or because of some other reason, have the chance to get involved.

As I circulated, I listened to an argument in one group about part of what Hal had written. "I know for sure that there are 12 tiles in the bag. There are 6 red, 4 blue, and 2 yellow." he read.

"You can't know that," Jason challenged, "you only know that there were 12 trials."

"You can only know that there is at least 1 red, 1 blue, and 1 yellow," Gretchen added.

"But there were 6 red, 4 blue, and 2 yellow," Hal said.

"They could have drawn the same tile out more than once," Jason countered.

"Or maybe there were lots more reds," Jesse said, "but they only got picked 6 times. You can't tell."

Finally Hal gave in. I'm not sure if his understanding had shifted or if he had responded to peer pressure. In either case, the discussion gave him the opportunity to reconsider his ideas.

Another group was talking about Julia's conjecture. She had written: "*I think that there are probably more red tiles than blue tiles, and more blue tiles than yellow tiles. There are probably about 5–7 red tiles, 3–5 blue, and 1–3 yellow tiles.*"

"How do you know that?" Joe asked.

"I don't know for sure," Julia answered, "but it could be."

"I don't think that's right," Matt said, "because then there could be 5 red tiles and 5 blue tiles, and there probably isn't the same of each."

"Well," Julia answered, "I meant if there were 5 red tiles, there would be 3 blue tiles."

"I still don't think you can say that," Joe answered.

"I know what she means," Sasha intervened. "She's just giving 'about' amounts."

When I called the class to attention for a discussion, I wrote "For sure" and "Probably true" on the board and asked the students for statements that their groups agreed on. Many of the students were willing to offer their thoughts.

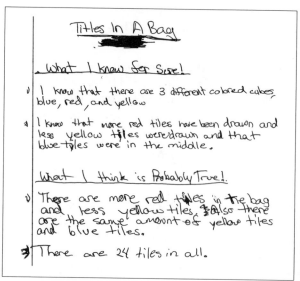

Two handwritten student worksheets:

Worksheet 1:

Titles In A Bag

What I know for Sure!

1) I know that there are 3 different colored cubes, blue, red, and yellow

2) I know that more red tiles have been drawn and less yellow tiles were drawn and that blue tiles were in the middle.

What I think is Probably True!.

1) There are more red tiles in the bag and less yellow tiles. Also there are the same amount of yellow tiles and blue tiles.

3) There are 24 tiles in all.

Worksheet 2:

MATH HOMEWORK
PART I
TILES IN A BAG
What I Know for Sure

I know that there are, at the very least, 3 tiles in the bag. I know that there is at least 1 yellow tile, 1 red tile, and one blue tile.

What I Think is Probably True

I think that there are probably more red tiles than blue tiles, and more blue tiles than yellow tiles. There are probably about 5-7 red tiles, 3-5 blue, and 1-3 yellow tiles.

Students were told that 12 samples from a bag of tiles resulted in 6 red, 4 blue, and 2 yellow tiles. For homework, they wrote what they knew for sure and what they thought was probably true.

We wound up with three statements on the "For sure" list. One was offered by Gretchen. "We know that there is at least 1 red, 1 blue, and 1 yellow," she said.

Another was reported by Robbie. "There are 12 draws," he said. "There are more red than the rest, and there are more blue than yellow."

Jason said, "Out of the 12 trials, ½ was red, ⅓ was blue, and ⅙ was yellow."

There were more statements for the "Probably true" list.

"There are probably more red than yellow or blue," Alison reported.

"There are probably more blue than yellow," Robbie added.

"There are probably only three colors," Jay said.

"But there could be more colors," Jesse said.

"Yes, but there are probably only three," Jay countered. The class sentiment supported Jay's view.

Michael said, "You could say that probably yellow could be ⅙ of the tiles in the bag, blue could be ⅓, and red could be ½."

"There's probably more than 1 red in the bag," Tami said.

"Well, what was in the bag?" Hal finally asked.

"I didn't have a bag in mind," I said, "I only had the results of 12 samples in mind." This statement resulted in a outbreak of protests.

"Wait, wait," I said to interrupt their complaints. "Sampling is used in real life because no one knows what the whole population really looks like. It's a way to make a reasonable prediction. If you knew the whole story, you wouldn't need to take samples."

"I don't get it," Sasha said.

"You hear on the news that some percent of the people are in favor of a new law," I said. "Everyone in the country wasn't polled. A sample was taken, a large enough sample so that the prediction is reliable."

Most of the students were satisfied with this response.

Final Thoughts

Studying probability presents students with a view of mathematics that differs in character from much of their other math learning. Students' previous experiences have led them to conclude that math problems usually have answers that can be figured out exactly. When they engage in probability experiments and simulations, however, they collect and use real data. Uncertainty and variability exist. Students are challenged to make sense of situations when they can't be totally sure about outcomes.

In these sorts of activities, the students are experiencing mathematics in an authentic way. They collect data, organize it, and interpret it to test their conjectures. By so doing, they gain experience with the related area of statistics.

Also, a new and exciting element of exploration is brought into lessons when the teacher doesn't have the answer or is not totally certain about what will occur. I've found this to contribute to students' interest and motivation.

As with any area of learning, students' understanding about probability needs to grow over time. I planned to give the students many experiences throughout the year through which they could further their understanding. To help me gauge what they currently knew, I asked them to write about what they had learned from these experiences.

ACTIVITIES WITH RATIO, PROPORTION, AND FRACTIONS

Students entering middle school have already had several years of instruction about fractions. They've been taught to name fractional parts; find fractional equivalents; and add, subtract, multiply, and divide with fractions. Still, middle-school teachers find that students are often confused about fractions. Their skills are weak, and their understanding is limited.

The activities in this chapter engage middle-school students with fractions through measuring activities using Cuisenaire Rods. The explorations do not have the honing of fraction skills as their exclusive or even primary goal. Instead, students are given concrete situations in which they apply fraction concepts and skills. They're asked to think about fractions and reason with them and discuss and explain their ideas.

This chapter is best read with Cuisenaire Rods at hand. Doing the activities with the rods is helpful for following the students' reasoning processes.

Three class periods with seventh and eighth graders are described. For each activity, the class was organized so that students worked in pairs. On the first day, students found the pairs of rods that show the fractional relationships of halves, thirds, fourths, and so on, up to tenths. In the second period, students investigated the relationships between the lengths of other pairs of rods. In the third period, they were presented with a measurement problem that involved them with ratio and proportion.

The class discussions in the second and third class periods revealed a wide spread in the students' understandings, from students who had a confident grasp of concepts to those who were in a muddle of confusion. This diversity, which is typical in middle-school classes, presented quite a challenge for teaching the lessons.

Videotape   "Fractions with Cuisenaire Rods" on Part 2 and "Ratio and Proportion with Cuisenaire Rods" on Part 1 of *Mathematics for Middle School* show the actual lessons that took place in the second and third class periods.

Day 1

"Prove with the rods that the yellow rod is half as long as the orange rod," I said to begin the first lesson. This was easy for the students. Most put 2 yellow rods end to end to show they matched an orange. Some put 1 yellow on top of an orange and were satisfied by eyeballing that it was half.

I then presented them with a problem. "Find all the other pairs of rods," I said, "for which one is half as long as the other. Again, prove each with the rods. Leave the pairs of rods on your desk so you can refer to them again."

This didn't take the students very long to do. There are five pairs of rods that show halves, including the yellow and orange rods. When I saw by the arrangements on their desks that most of the students had found all the pairs, I called the class to attention.

"What did you notice when you were doing this?" I asked.

"It was easy," Nathan said.

"We could only find five," Yvette said.

"It skips every other one," Randy said. He had arranged 10 rods in a staircase and found halves for every other rod in the sequence.

"You can use the red and purple rods twice," Jorge said.

There were no other comments. I then showed the students how to write two mathematical sentences to describe the relationship between the orange and yellow rods. The students had already been introduced to the standard abbreviations: w (white), r (red), g (light green), p (purple), y (yellow), d (dark green), k (black), n (brown), e (blue), o (orange).

"One sentence starts with yellow," I said, "and the other starts with orange." I wrote on the chalkboard:

$$y = \tfrac{1}{2} o$$
$$o = 2y$$

"Raise your hand if you can tell two sentences that describe the relationship between another pair of rods," I said.

I called on Eva. She gave me two sentences to relate the red and purple rods. Then Cicero gave me the sentences for light green and dark green. I continued until I had sentences for each of the five pairs.

"Now compare the blue and light-green rods," I then said, "and talk with the person next to you about two sentences you can write to describe the relationship between them."

I gave them a few minutes to do this and then called on Kim to report. "⅓ of blue equals light green," she said, "and 3 light greens equals 1 blue." The others nodded their assent.

I then gave them an investigation to do with their partners. "Find all the other pairs of rods for which one is ⅓ of the other," I said, "and write two sentences to describe each. Then do the same for fourths, fifths, sixths, and so on, up to tenths. When you and your partner think you've found all that are possible, check with the others at your table to see if you agree."

The students got to work. Pairs worked differently. Some looked for fractional relationships in an orderly way, focusing first on finding the thirds, then the fourths, then the fifths, and so on. Others chose one rod, such as the orange, and compared it to all the other rods, looking for fractional relationships. Still others seemed to have no system but just rummaged through the rods and recorded relationships as they noticed them.

Kim and David investigate the fractional relationships between pairs of Cuisenaire Rods.

Students did not have difficulty with this assignment. However, as they worked, several asked me how many sentences they were supposed to have in all. My stock reply was, "Deciding when you have found them all is part of the problem you're to solve."

In a class discussion, students reported the different methods they used. Only those who had proceeded in an organized way were able to explain why they were sure they had found all that were possible.

Day 2

The second lesson was an extension of the first experience. I asked students to investigate the relationship between five pairs of rods and record two mathematical sentences to describe each. I wrote the five pairs on the chalkboard:

1. red and light green
2. red and blue
3. purple and orange
4. purple and yellow
5. orange and dark green

Some students worked more quickly than others. As pairs finished, I asked that they continue with any two rods of their choosing. When everyone had either finished or gone as far as they could, I called the class to attention for a discussion.

All students had found the first two easy. Liz reported the two sentences she and Khalil had written for the first problem. "Red is ⅔ of light green," she said, "and light green is 1½ reds." I wrote on the board:

$$r = \tfrac{2}{3}\,g \qquad g = 1\tfrac{1}{2}\,r$$

"Explain how you figured that," I said.

"It takes 3 whites to make a light green," Liz said, "and only 2 whites to make a red. So red is 2 out of the 3, and that's ⅔." There were nods of assent from other students.

"What about the other sentence?" I asked.

Khalil explained. "Well, if you put 2 reds next to the light green," he said, "it's too long. Only 1½ would fit."

"Does anyone have any other thoughts about these relationships?" I asked.

Phi raised his hand. "I got the same," he said, "but I matched the light green with a red and a white. And since I know that white is half of red, then light green has to be 1½ red."

There were no other comments, so I went on the second relationship. Alex reported for him and Nam. "Orange is worth 2½ purples," he said, "because it takes 2 purples and a red to make an orange, and red is half of purple." I wrote on the board:

$$o = 2\tfrac{1}{2}\,p$$

Alex continued with the other sentence. "And purple is ⁴⁄₁₀ of orange," he said, "because if you use the whites, purple is 4 white and orange is 10 whites."

1. $g = \tfrac{1}{2}\,r$ $r = \tfrac{2}{3}\,g$

2. $e = 4\tfrac{1}{2}\,r$ $r = \tfrac{2}{9}\,e$

3. $o = 2\tfrac{1}{2}\,p$ $p = \tfrac{4}{10}\,o$

4. $y = 1\tfrac{1}{4}\,p$ $p = \tfrac{4}{5}\,y$

5. $o = 1\tfrac{2}{3}\,d$ $d = \tfrac{3}{5}\,o$

6. $o = 1\tfrac{1}{9}\,e$ $c = \tfrac{9}{10}\,o$

7. $o = 10\,w$ $w = \tfrac{1}{10}\,o$

8. $b = 1\tfrac{1}{7}\,k$ $k = \tfrac{7}{9}\,b$

Alex and Nam had time to investigate relationships between three additional pairs of rods.

I wrote on the board:

$$p = \tfrac{4}{10}\, o$$

Eric raised his hand. "We got $p = \tfrac{2}{5}\, o$," he said for him and Tamika. "But it's the same thing. We just measured with reds, not whites."

I wrote on the board:

$$p = \tfrac{2}{5}\, o$$

"Explain to the class how you measured," I said.

"You can make an orange with 5 reds," Eric said, "and a purple with 2 reds. So purple is 2 out of 5, and that's $\tfrac{2}{5}$."

Not all the students in the class had the confidence and clarity projected by those students who were reporting. Class presentations by confident students can help those who are less sure. These students present another perspective and suggest ways to rethink ideas.

The discussions on the next two problems continued in a similar way. A great deal of confusion was expressed, however, in the discussion of number 5. Darshana raised her hand to report the two sentences she and Jon wrote to describe the relationship between the orange and dark-green rods. I recorded what she reported on the board:

$$o = 1\tfrac{3}{4} \qquad d = \tfrac{2}{10}$$

"But o equals $1\tfrac{3}{4}$ doesn't tell about the relationship between the two rods," I said.

Darshana hastily offered a correction. "Oh, I mean that one whole dark green fits in an orange and $\tfrac{3}{4}$ of another dark green," she said.

"Can you explain how you got that?" I asked.

"We put a dark green next to the orange and then another, and only $\tfrac{3}{4}$ of the other fit on it," she said to explain her first sentence. "Then we put 10 whites under the orange, and there were two extras to the end of the dark greens, so dark green is $\tfrac{2}{10}$ of orange." I changed her sentences to read:

$$o = 1\tfrac{3}{4}\, d \qquad d = \tfrac{2}{10}\, o$$

I knew that these sentences weren't correct. Rather than deal with this now, however, I decided to hear what other students had to say. Jimmy had his hand raised.

"I don't think it should be $\tfrac{2}{10}$," he said. "I think it should be d equals $\tfrac{3}{5}\, o$." I wrote this on the board under what Darshana had reported:

$$o = 1\tfrac{3}{4}\, d \qquad d = \tfrac{2}{10}\, o$$
$$d = \tfrac{3}{5}\, o$$

Jimmy's answer was correct, but he didn't seem totally sure himself of what he had reported.

Eric had a contribution. "I think it should be d equals $1\tfrac{2}{3}\, o$," he said. I added this to the board:

$$o = 1\tfrac{3}{4}\, d \qquad d = \tfrac{2}{10}\, o$$
$$d = \tfrac{3}{5}\, o$$
$$d = 1\tfrac{2}{3}\, o$$
$$d = \tfrac{6}{10}\, o$$

Eric went on to explain his reasoning. "Dark green is 6 long and orange is 10," he said. "When you put another dark green on it, it takes only 4 whites, so we simplified 1⁴⁄₆ to 1⅔." Eric's thinking was correct, but he had the colors reversed. He reported d equals 1⅔ o, but it should have been o equals 1⅔ d. Still I didn't comment. I asked for other ideas. Phi raised his hand.

"We got one kind of like Jimmy's," he reported for him and Lemuel, "except we wrote d equals ⁶⁄₁₀ o." I added this to the board:

$$o = 1\tfrac{3}{4}\,d \qquad d = \tfrac{2}{10}\,o$$
$$d = \tfrac{3}{5}\,o$$
$$d = 1\tfrac{2}{3}\,o$$
$$d = \tfrac{6}{10}\,o$$

"How is that like Jimmy's?" I asked.

"Because if you divide the numbers by 2," he said, "then 2 into 6 is 3, and 2 into 10 is 5, so ⁶⁄₁₀ and ⅗ are the same."

Darshana then raised her hand. "I think my answer is wrong," she said. "I found out what happened."

"Explain what you think," I said.

"I think the last answer, ⁶⁄₁₀, makes sense," she said.

"Why do you think ⁶⁄₁₀ makes sense?" I asked.

Darshana hesitated. "I don't know," she replied. "I just think it's right."

"Phi," I said, "perhaps it would help others if you explained your thinking." Phi was willing. He came to the board and demonstrated with the magnetic rods. He showed that 10 white rods made an orange and that a dark green was 6 white rods.

"So dark green is ⁶⁄₁₀ of orange," he said.

"Does that make sense?" I asked Darshana. She nodded yes, but I wasn't totally convinced that Darshana understood why Phi's answer made sense.

Loc had his hand raised. Loc doesn't often volunteer to speak in class because his English is limited. I asked him what he would like to add.

"I don't agree with the first one," he said. "I think 1¾ should be 1⅔." I added another sentence to the board.

$$o = 1\tfrac{3}{4}\,d \qquad d = \tfrac{2}{10}\,o$$
$$o = 1\tfrac{2}{3}\,d \qquad d = \tfrac{3}{5}\,o$$
$$d = 1\tfrac{2}{3}\,o$$
$$d = \tfrac{6}{10}\,o$$

Loc's suggestion corrected the error I had noticed with what Eric had reported a little while before.

It's hard when you're teaching and you know some students are getting it and others aren't. I've come to understand that partial understanding and periods of confusion are natural to the learning process. I know that learning doesn't always happen in forty-three-minute periods and, for some students, not even over several days.

What's crucial for teachers to keep in mind, I think, is that students must construct their own understandings. I let the confusion stand for now and planned to return to the investigation in another way. Rather than explaining for the sake of efficiency, teachers must continue to involve students so they can uncover mathematical relationships for themselves.

Day 3

I began the third lesson by gathering the students around one desk to see how many light green rods were needed to measure across it. I began measuring and stopped after I had placed 5 rods.

"How many light-green rods do you think are needed to measure across the desk?" I asked. I gave the students time to look and estimate. Then I called on Jorge.

"About 20," he said.

"Why do you think that?" I asked.

"If you put three times like that again," he said, referring to the rods I had already placed on the desk, "then you would get 20, because that would be 4 times 5."

Kim had a different estimate. "15," she said. "It looks like three sets of 5 would reach across."

"Does anyone have a different idea?" I asked.

Craig answered, "About 20," he said, "because of the way your fingers are. It looks like it would go across four times."

"I'll put 5 more rods down," I said, "and see what that extra information tells you." I continued measuring with the rods until there were 10 on the desk.

"Now what do you think?" I asked.

Cicero answered. "I think 18," he said. "One more set would be too much. It looks like only 8 more will fit."

I then continued measuring. It took 20 light-green rods in all.

"When you were making your estimates," I said to the class, "you were using ideas in math called *ratio* and *proportion*. Return to your seats now, and I'm going to give you some ratio and proportion problems to work on with partners."

This introduction served to give baseline information that the students would now use to figure how many rods of other lengths it would take to measure across the desktop. Before giving them problems to solve independently, I posed one for a class discussion.

"Because I now know that it takes 20 light-green rods to measure across the desk," I said, "I think it would take 10 dark-green rods. Who can explain why I think that makes sense?" Though the students had previous experience with the rods, I showed them that 2 light-green rods were equal in length to 1 dark-green rod.

I chose Frank to respond. He seemed to understand but had an extremely difficult time explaining his thinking. "Because if it takes 20 light-green rods," he began, "and it takes 2 light greens to make 1 dark green, then you just subtract . . . or you take away 2 light greens and change it with a dark green."

"I think I understand what you mean," I responded to Frank, "but try and explain it again."

This time Frank said, "You could substitute 1 dark green for 2 light greens, and it would only take 10 dark greens instead of 20 light greens." Though he stumbled on the word *substitute*, his explanation was clearer and more succinct.

I took this opportunity to talk about the importance of their explaining their reasoning. "I know that sometimes it's hard to find the words to express your ideas," I said. "That's why I try and give you as many chances as possible to explain your ideas. You need practice, and the more opportunities you have to explain, the easier it will become."

Frank flashed a smile of relief. He's a willing student for whom words don't come easily. My statement seemed to validate the importance of his effort.

I then posed the problem for the class to do in pairs. "Your problem is to figure out about how many red, white, and blue rods it would take to measure across the desk," I said. "Don't actually measure, but use the information about the light-green and dark-green rods. Record your answers and explain your reasoning for each. I'm interested in how you arrive at answers that make sense to you."

The students got engaged quickly and stayed involved. I've found that when students are comfortable with a material and understand the problem, they're willing to take on a challenge. That was the case with this activity.

I asked those pairs who finished more quickly to figure out how many purple rods it would take. When all the students had found solutions for the red, white, and blue rods, I called the class to attention to discuss their work.

"How many blue rods are needed to measure across the desk?" I asked to begin the discussion.

Craig answered first. "6⅔," he said. "There's 3 light greens fit in a blue, and 3 times 6 is 18, and then there isn't room for a full rod, only 2 light greens, and that's ⅔."

Nathan had a different answer. "About 6," he said. "We compared blues and light greens and found 20 light greens fit on 6 blues."

Then Kim reported. "6¾," she said. "We laid them out. We didn't have enough blue, so we used others to piece it together."

"So we have three different answers," I said. "They're all close, but I need to hear more from you to better understand your thinking and your methods. What about the red rod? How many of those stretch across the desk?"

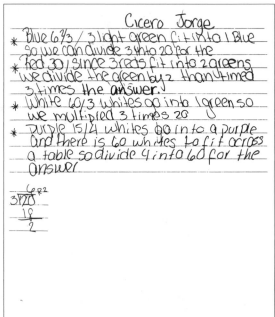

Students' papers reveal their different ways of reasoning.

Yvette explains how she and Elena figured how many red rods it took to measure across the table.

All those that reported this time gave the same answer. However, their reasoning differed. Melissa answered first.

"We figured 30," she said, "because it takes 10 dark-green rods, and it takes 3 red rods to make a dark green, so 3 times 10 equals 30."

Jorge used a different approach. "3 reds fit into 2 light greens," he said, "so we divided the light greens by 2 and multiplied by 3."

Yvette reported next. "4½ times 6⅔ equals 9 over 2 times 20 over 3, which equals 30," she said.

I was stumped. Yvette and her partner Elisa both seemed confident, but I couldn't track their thinking.

"That's very fancy," I said. "Explain it once more and let me try and follow your reasoning. First, where did the 4½ come from."

"3 light greens equal 4 reds with ½ a red more," Yvette explained. I used magnetic Cuisenaire Rods to show that relationship on the board.

"Then we multiplied by 6⅔," she said.

"Where did that come from?" I asked.

"The blue rod," Yvette answered.

Their reasoning made sense to me now, since 3 light-green rods are equal in length to a blue rod. However, I wasn't sure that the others in the class were following their logic.

"Raise your hand," I said to the class, "if you didn't really understand the explanation Yvette and Elisa gave." About half the class raised their hands.

"It's hard to follow someone else's reasoning," I said. "What's important is to figure things out for yourself using processes that make sense to you." Whenever possible, I try and reinforce for the students that understanding what they're doing is what's most important to me. By letting them know this, I shift the goal of math lessons from merely getting right answers to being able to explain and justify what they've found.

Final Thoughts

Gaps in the students' understandings became evident in these activities. A difficulty at the middle-school level is that the understandings in a class are often extremely diverse. A further complication is that there isn't a clearly defined continuum of understanding in a class from students who know little to those who know a great deal. More typically, individual students have developed understanding of different bits of the total picture.

For many students, the emphasis of their prior experience with fractions has been on memorizing and practicing rules and algorithms as separate and often unrelated procedures. I've found that breaking a subject into separate parts and helping students learn about those parts doesn't necessarily help them put the whole picture together. It's like giving students puzzle pieces without giving them a clue about what the picture will look like when it's assembled. The confusion that students revealed in these classes indicated to me the danger of a bits-and-pieces approach to teaching.

I think that students need experiences with fractions that emphasize seeing relationships, making connections, and learning about their use. I try to provide this experience by finding activities that are accessible to all students, so that those with limited understandings can engage, contribute, and have the opportunity to make connections between what they know and what they haven't yet learned. In addition, the activities need to be rich enough to entice and challenge students who understand more. The activities in this chapter seemed to provide this balance.

When teaching, the temptation to revert to teaching by telling emerges when students aren't understanding. I've come to ignore that impulse, however. Though teaching by telling may seem more efficient, it doesn't respect or support the importance of students' constructing their understanding for themselves.

The choices I made during these classes certainly weren't the only possible responses in these situations. A discussion with colleagues about teaching alternatives that could have been used when the students' confusion surfaced would be a beneficial way to explore teaching alternatives and options.

MEASURING ANGLES

The study of geometry helps students connect mathematics to the real world. Students who have or are able to develop spatial sense are better able to interpret and appreciate the world of shapes in which we live. To build students' spatial understandings, school experiences should engage them in visualizing, drawing, measuring, constructing, and exploring relationships among geometric figures.

The study of angles is one topic in the area of geometry. From previous experiences in math classes and informal experiences out of school, middle-school students generally have learned that angles are the shapes of corners and that they can be pointy, wide, or square. For the most part, however, they have had limited experience with exploring the properties of angles, relating them to other geometric figures, and learning how to measure them. The lessons in this chapter model ways to provide students with hands-on experiences for exploring angles using Pattern Blocks, mirrors, paper folding and tearing, and protractors.

The activities presented in this chapter help students learn that the size of an angle is a measure of rotation. They are introduced to the idea that a right angle is one-fourth revolution, that a straight angle is one-half revolution, and that any angle can be measured by comparing it to a complete revolution. They are also introduced to the idea that degrees are the standard measure of angles, that a complete revolution measures 360°, and that 1° is ⅟₃₆₀ revolution.

Students usually are taught how to use a protractor as the standard tool for measuring angles. Students learning to use protractors to measure angles sometimes get confused by the two scales of numbers. "Which number do I use?" is a question they commonly ask. The answer should be obvious as only one of the numbers makes sense when eyeballing the size of the angle. However, when students' understanding of angles is weak, they often lose sight of the meaning of the measures and are not clear about what makes sense. Some students learn to use a protractor in the same way they learned to do long division or divide fractions, by following an algorithm by rote rather than by reasoning.

In these lessons, the protractor is introduced after the students have had a series of concrete experiences with angles. The students use hinged mirrors to measure the angles of Pattern Blocks. They then use the mirrors to construct angles of different sizes and fold and tear paper to explore other angles. Finally, the students are given protractors. Working in pairs, they figure out for themselves how to use the protractor to measure angles and write directions for its use. The lessons were taught to eighth graders.

Videotape "Angles with Pattern Blocks and Hinged Mirrors" appears in Part 1 of *Mathematics for Middle School*. In a previous lesson, the students figured out the degrees in each angle of the Pattern Blocks. This lesson shows them working in groups of four to construct angles of different sizes. In a summarizing class discussion, each group reports one angle it constructed and explains the method used.

Day 1

"We're going to be studying about angles," I said to begin the class. "To start, I'm interested in finding out what you already know about angles."

"They're like the corners of things," Jerry said. "They have something to do with triangles and rectangles."

"They're lines like the hands on a clock," Jenny offered.

"They have degrees," Erica said.

Patty raised her hand. "Isn't an angle like not straight up and down? You know, slanted?" I asked Patty to draw on the overhead what she meant. She drew an acute angle with one horizontal leg.

"That's an acute angle," Paul said.

"What do you know about acute angles?" I asked Paul.

"They're kind of pointy," he answered, "not real open." I wrote "acute angle" next to the angle Patty had drawn.

"Acute angles have less than 90°," Jeremia said.

"I know about right angles," Russell said. "They're like L's." I drew one on the overhead and labeled it.

You know when you're skiing, and you turn all the way around?" Cheryl asked. "Isn't that like 360°?"

"Yes," I answered.

"It's the same on a skateboard," Herman said. "You do 360s and 180s." This resulted in some comments about skateboard techniques. I drew the class back to attention.

"Does anyone know anything else about angles," I asked, "or have another question to ask?"

"Does a right angle have 90°?" Jennie asked.

"Yes," I answered. Several students were nodding in agreement. "Can anyone explain why a right angle is 90°?"

Patty remembered learning about that. "I think it has to do with what Cheryl said about 360° and dividing it up." Though others knew that a right angle measured 90°, no one else had any idea about why.

The students brought a variety of ideas to this discussion. Most seemed to have the general understanding that an angle is the shape of a corner. Fewer, however, seemed to know about measuring the size of an angle.

The class gathers together to learn how to use hinged mirrors to measure the angles of the Pattern Blocks.

I then told the class what I had planned for the next few days. "You're going to be exploring angles in several different ways this week," I said. "Today I'll show you how to measure all the different-sized angles of the Pattern Blocks using a pair of hinged mirrors. For this activity, you'll be using the information that 360° makes a complete circle, as Cheryl and Herman said." If Cheryl and Herman hadn't come forth with their examples, I would have told the students that there are 360° in one complete rotation. This is a fact, an arbitrary piece of information, that students need to know.

I gathered the students around one group's table to show them how to use the hinged mirrors to measure the angles of the Pattern Blocks. The class had enough previous experience with Pattern Blocks that they didn't need time to explore them. They were familiar with the shapes and colors.

I placed a corner of an orange square into the corner of a pair of hinged mirrors and closed the sides so that they were touching the sides of the square and the square was firmly nestled. I had students do the same with three other pairs of mirrors so that more of the class could see.

"What do you see when you look into the hinged mirrors?" I asked.

Alisa was positioned so she could see. "There are four squares," she said. "Three in the mirrors and the one on the table." There was much interest among the students to explore with the mirrors. I put four squares on the desk, and Alisa arranged them to show what she saw.

"As Cheryl and Herman said," I continued, "it takes 360° to make a complete circle. Putting the square in the mirrors shows that it takes the corners of four squares to fill a complete rotation. So one square corner is one-fourth of 360°." Some of the students understood this immediately; others looked perplexed.

"How much is one-fourth of 360°?" I asked. Some students figured quickly that it was 90°.

"So a square corner, which is called a *right angle*, equals 90°," I said.

"Why is it called a *right angle*?" Russell asked.

"I don't know," I said. "That might be a topic of interest for someone to research. I've never thought about it."

"Maybe it's a left angle if it goes like a backward L," Jennie said.

"No," I said, "a square corner is a right angle no matter what position it's in." I then brought the students' attention back to the Pattern Blocks.

"Notice that all four angles of the squares are the same size," I said. "They're congruent. Some of the Pattern Blocks have all congruent angles and some don't."

Some students called out what they noticed. "They're all the same on the green triangle." "On the yellow block, too." "They're different on the blue diamond." I had the students seated at the table take one of each of the six blocks and sort them into two groups: those with all angles congruent and those with different-sized angles.

I then used the blue rhombus to model what to do with blocks with angles of more than one size. "You can place the blue block in the hinged mirrors two different ways," I said. "Which vertex you put in the corner of the mirrors determines the reflection you see."

"What's *vertex*?" Jennie asked.

"It's another word for the corner of a polygon or the point of an angle," I said. I made a note to myself to use the word as often as possible so the students would become familiar with its use.

There were pleased reactions when the students saw the pattern made by putting the smaller angle into the mirrors. "Ooh, that's pretty." "It's like a star." "How many do you see?" Kristin, also seated at the table, built what she saw.

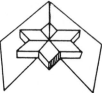

"Since it takes six blocks to complete a rotation," I said, "each of those angles is one-sixth of 360°." A few students quickly did the division in their heads.

"But then you need to figure out the size of the other angle as well. To do this, position the block with the wide corner nestled in the hinged mirrors," I said. I did this with the block.

"Go back to your seats now," I then said, "and I'll give you specific directions about what you're to do."

When the students were seated, I told them they were to figure out how many degrees there were in each angle of the blocks. "Use the hinged mirrors as I showed you," I said. "Build what you see and then draw it." I showed on the overhead what they should draw for the square.

"Then draw a circle to show the complete rotation," I continued, "and figure out how much the angle measures. To write degrees, you use a little zero." I showed them how to do this.

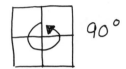

"You may find it easier to trace the Pattern Blocks than to make a sketch," I added.

I then gave directions about materials. "You and your partner will each need Pattern Blocks, a pair of hinged mirrors, and a piece of 12- by 18-inch newsprint for recording," I said. I keep the Pattern Blocks for the class in small plastic bags. I distributed the contents of five complete buckets into eight bags. Also, I hinged small plastic mirrors (about 2 by 3 inches) with strapping tape, so there was a pair for every two students.

"Send someone to get supplies for both pairs at your table," I said. "Because you've never explored with the hinged mirrors before, take some time to do so. But be sure to start on the assignment by five after the hour." That gave them about seven minutes for exploring. I've learned that students need time to satisfy their curiosity about a new material. Setting a time limit honors that need while reminding them of their task.

Once the students began working on the task, some confusion surfaced. I helped several pairs who hadn't been able to see very well during the demonstration. A few other pairs could figure how many blocks it took to make 360° but couldn't remember what to do then. Gradually, the groups figured out what to do, and the room settled into the hum of purposeful work. The students' interest was high.

The tan rhombus posed a problem for the students. Placing the small angle in the hinged mirrors produces a star cluster of 12 blocks. This delighted students, and most were able to figure that the angle measured 30°. However, placing the larger angle in the hinged mirrors produces a reflection that's frustrating because it can't be built. Students had to find other ways to figure out its size.

Kristy and Erika found that the larger angle of the tan rhombus was equal to two angles of green triangles and the smaller angle of the tan rhombus. They added 120° and 30° to get 150°. They wrote: *"Two of the triangles and one tan rhombus fit in the angle."*

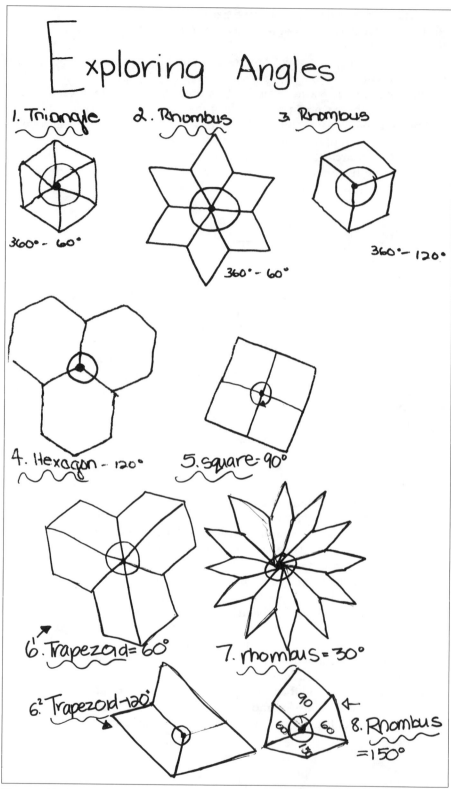

Exploring Angles

1. Triangle
360° - 60°

2. Rhombus
360° - 60°

3. Rhombus
360° - 120°

4. Hexagon - 120°

5. square - 90°

6.¹ Trapezoid = 60°

7. rhombus = 30°

6.² Trapezoid - 120°

8. Rhombus = 150°
90
60 60
15

Tami and Kelly noticed they had omitted the larger angle of the trapezoid and included it at the bottom of their paper.

Jenifer and Sarah proved that the angle measured 150° by seeing that the angle was the same size as the 30° angle and the large 120° angle of the red trapezoid combined.

Tami and Kelly showed that the orange square, two green triangles, and the large angle of the tan rhombus combined to make 360°.

The hinged mirrors aren't essential for this activity. It's possible to use just the blocks and see how many of each angle are needed to complete a 360° rotation. However, using the mirrors with the blocks is not only aesthetically pleasing and exciting for the students, it prepares them for the next day's activity.

I gave the students a homework assignment for that night. "Fold one corner of a piece of paper in half," I said. I modeled this for the class. "Trace the angle on a sheet of paper and record the number of degrees in it. Then fold the angle again, trace, and record the degrees. Continue until you can't fold the angle any more. Bring the paper you folded to class along with your recording sheet."

Days 2 and 3

I began class by having the students in their small groups compare the angles they traced for homework. I circulated and checked who had completed the assignment.

When I called the class to attention, I had one group report the sizes of the angles they had traced. They had angles of 45°, 22½°, and 11¼°. I recorded these on the overhead. The rest of the class indicated they had the same answers.

I noticed when I checked their assignments that students had folded angles from different-sized pieces of paper. I pointed this out to the class. "Though the sheets of paper you used were different sizes," I said, "you all recorded the same-sized angles." This led to a discussion about the size of angles. Patty's statement summarized the conversation.

"It's how pointy that counts," she said, "not how long."

Next I drew intersecting perpendicular lines on the overhead.

"Can anyone tell me how many degrees there are in each of these angles?" I asked. Most of the students raised their hands. I called on Russell.

"It's 90°," he said.

"How do you know that?" I asked him.

"Because I know an L shape is 90°," he said, repeating what he had offered yesterday in class.

Jerry raised his hand. "I imagined a circle," he said.

"How did that help you?" I asked. Jerry shrugged his shoulders. Some students have difficulty expressing their ideas. Jenny helped out.

"A circle has 360°, so you just divide by 4," she said.

Rochelle had a different explanation. "Anytime you see a line going straight up and down, and another one going straight across," he said, "you know that it's 90°."

I turned the transparency diagonally so the lines looked like an X. "Are they still 90°?" I asked. For a moment, the class was silent, and then students began to talk. "They're just on a slant." "But it doesn't look right." "Their size wasn't changed, just the tilt." "Oh, yeah, it's still the same."

I added two more lines to my figure, bisecting each of the angles.

"What about the size of these angles?" I asked. "Talk this over in your groups." I gave them a moment to do this, then called on Crystal.

"45°," she said. "We divided 8 into 360°."

"It's the same as one of the angles on our homework," Stacy said.

"This is just like the Pattern Blocks," Ron said, a bit impatiently.

I then explained the exploration the students were to do next. "Today you'll investigate angles of other sizes," I began. "You'll use the hinged mirrors, Pattern Blocks, and a sheet like this on which I've drawn a dot and a line." I showed a sample sheet to the class.

"First I'll give you some time to explore what the hinged mirrors produce on the paper with the dot and the line," I continued. "Place the hinged mirrors so the dot is inside and near the vertex of the angle. Also, make sure the mirrors cross the line." I showed them what I meant.

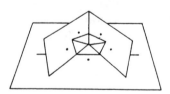

"The size of the angle the mirrors make determines whether you see 3 dots, 4 dots, 5 dots, or more," I said. "Also, the shapes made by the reflections of the lines change. Look at the angle of the hinged mirrors for different numbers of dots and different shapes and see what you can discover."

The students were intrigued with what they saw. Sam, who rarely is interested in class, got involved with making the angle of the hinged mirrors smaller and smaller. "I see 20 dots!" he said. Alisa and Sara also got interested. They claimed they saw 24 dots. Soon there was an informal contest. Lisa and Patty counted 36 dots. "That's a 10° angle," Lisa announced.

After a few minutes, I called the class back to attention and explained what they now were to do. "The next activity is called Weird Angles," I said. "You are to use hinged mirrors, Pattern Blocks, the dot and the line, and folded paper to create six 'weird' angles. Construct each angle by tracing and then describe how you made it."

I modeled an example for them. "If I position the mirrors so I see 5 dots and trace inside the mirrors to draw an angle," I said, "I can figure its size by dividing 5 into 360°." I did this for the class.

"Then if I put the 45° angle from the folded paper adjacent to it and trace," I continued, "I've made an angle that is 72° plus 45°, so it measures 119°. That's one way to construct an angle using the hinged mirrors and folded paper."

The class seemed interested but unsure. "I could also use one of the Pattern Blocks with either the 72° angle or the folded angle," I said, "to make a different-sized angle." I modeled this for the class as well.

"Do not construct any of the angles you've already found," said. I wrote on the overhead:

Do not construct 30°, 60°, 90°, 120°, 150°, 45°, 22½°, or 11¼°.

"Also," I continued, "though you can help each other and talk about what you're doing, each of you should individually draw angles on your own paper."

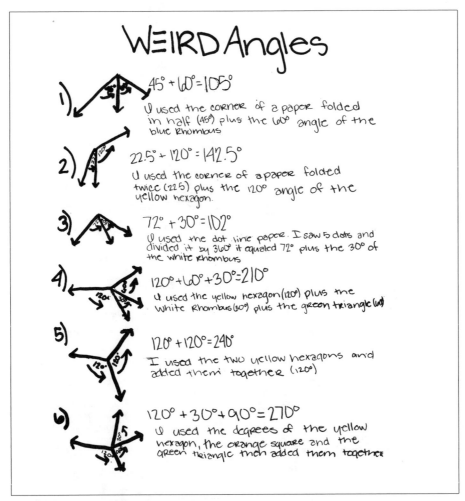

Students' papers showed they used a variety of methods to construct angles.

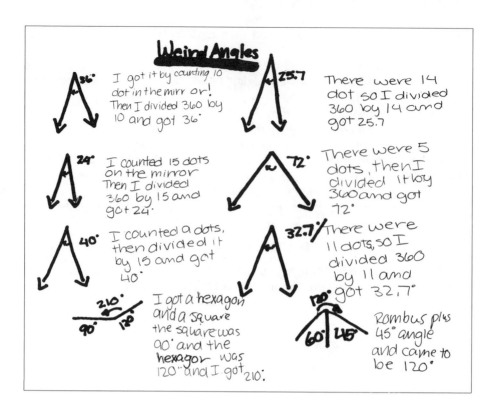

Weird Angles

36° — I got it by counting 10 dot in the mirr or! Then I divided 360 by 10 and got 36°

25.7 — There were 14 dot so I divided 360 by 14 and got 25.7

24° — I counted 15 dots on the mirror Then I divided 360 by 15 and got 24°

72° — There were 5 dots, then I divided it by 360 and got 72°

40° — I counted 9 dots, then divided it by 15 and got 40°

32.7% — There were 11 dots, so I divided 360 by 11 and got 32.7°

210° **90°** **120°** — I got a hexagon and a square the square was 90° and the hexagon was 120° and I got 210°

120° 60° 45° — Rombus plus 45° angle and came to be 120°

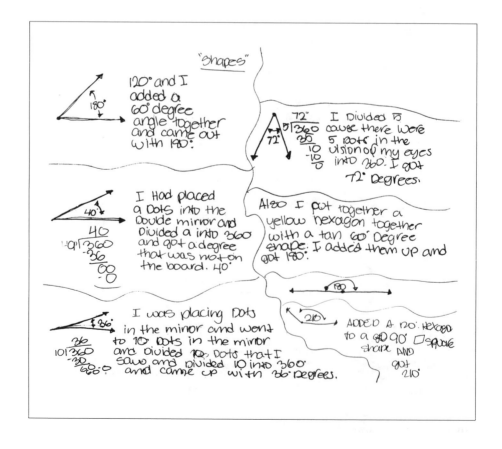

"shapes"

180° — 120° and I added a 60° degree angle together and came out with 180°.

$72°$ $5\overline{)360}$ — I Divided 5 couse there were 5 Dots in the vision of my eyes into 360. I got 72° Degrees.

$\begin{array}{r} 72 \\ 5\overline{)360} \\ \underline{35} \\ 10 \\ \underline{-10} \\ 0 \end{array}$

40° — I Had placed 9 Dots into the Double mirror and Divided 9 into 360 and got a degree that was not on the board. 40°

$\begin{array}{r} 40 \\ 40\overline{)360} \\ \underline{-36} \\ 00 \\ \underline{-0} \\ 0 \end{array}$

Also I put together a yellow hexagon together with a tan 60° Degree shape. I added them up and got 180°.

36° — I was placing Dots in the mirror and went to 10 Dots in the mirror and divided the Dots that I saw, and divided 10 into 360° and came up with 36° Degrees.

$\begin{array}{r} 36 \\ 10\overline{)360} \\ \underline{-30} \\ 60 \\ \underline{-60} \\ 0 \end{array}$

180

210° — ADDED A 120° HEXAGON to a old 90° □ SQUARE shape AND got 210°

Weird Angles

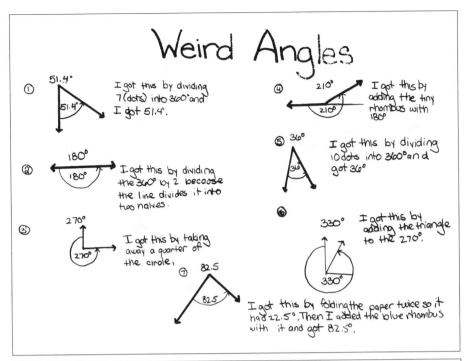

① 51.4°
51.4°
I got this by dividing 7 (dots) into 360° and I got 51.4°.

② 180°
180°
I got this by dividing the 360° by 2 becaose the line divides it into two halves.

③ 270°
270°
I got this by taking away a quarter of the circle.

④ 210°
210°
I got this by adding the tiny rhombus with 180°

⑤ 36°
36°
I got this by dividing 10 dots into 360° and got 36°

⑥ 330°
330°
I got this by adding the triangle to the 270°.

⑦ 82.5
82.5
I got this by folding the paper twice so it had 22.5°. Then I added the blue rhombus with it and got 82.5°.

Weird Angles

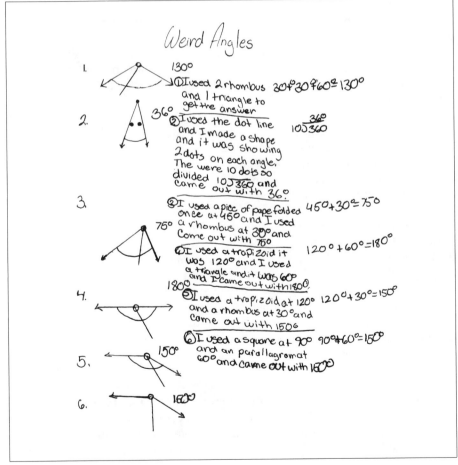

1. 130°
①I used 2 rhombus and 1 triangle to get the answer
30°+30°+60°=130°

2. 36°
②I used the dot line and I made a shape and it was showing 2 dots on each angle. The were 10 dots so divided 10⟌360 and came out with 36.
360
10⟌360

3. 75°
③I used a pice of pape folded once at 45° and I used a rhombus at 30° and come out with 75
45°+30°=75°

④I used a tropizoid it was 120° and I used a triangle and it was 60° and I came out with 180°.
120°+60°=180°

4. 180°
⑤I used a tropizoid at 120° and a rhombus at 30° and came out with 150°
120°+30°=150°

5. 150°
⑥I used a square at 90° and an parallagromat 60° and came out with 150°
90°+60°=150°

6. 150°

There was a fair amount of insecurity and confusion among the students when they got to work. Many students raised their hands for help, and I did as much troubleshooting as possible. Just before the end of the period, I asked who was still having difficulty. Ten students raised their hands. I wrote a list of their names.

The next day I had the students who weren't having difficulty get back to work and gathered the ten on my list. I showed them again what they were to do. All but two were able to get to work. I worked some more with the remaining two, and finally they were on their way.

One of the difficulties that arose was with angles greater than 180°. Students weren't accustomed to these, and some were unsure if they "really counted."

The period went smoothly. It was a good idea to call the activity Weird Angles. The students seemed to get confidence and energy from creating something they thought was unusual and mathematically important.

Day 4

To begin class the next day, I put the following two statements on the overhead:

1. The sum of the degrees of the three interior angles of a green block is 180°.
2. A straight line, or straight angle, measures 180°.

"Mathematicians believe these two statements to be true," I said. "Discuss them in your groups and describe in writing how you might prove one or both of them."

"What does *interior* mean?" Cuong asked.

"It means 'inside,' " I answered. "The interior angles are the angles inside the shape." I drew a few shapes on the overhead to illustrate. This seemed to satisfy Cuong.

After the groups had had discussion time, I had them report their thinking in a class discussion. There was agreement among the groups on how to verify the first statement. The reasoning from table 3 was typical: *Each angle is measured to be 60°. The triangle has three angles. If you times 60 by 3 you get 180°.*

Most groups explained the second statement in either of two ways. Table 4 wrote: *The straight line is 180° because a whole circle is 360°. If you divide 360° by 2 you will get 180°.*

Table 2 wrote: *If you put two 90° angles together, you get 180°.*

Table 1 presented a different explanation, however. They wrote: *You have a triangle. If you cut the top, the sides will fall down and form a 180° angle.* However, they weren't able to convince many of the others that their reasoning made sense.

I then showed the class an equilateral triangle I had drawn on a piece of construction paper. "This is the same shape as the green block," I said, "but it's larger. What can you say about the sum of the interior angles of this triangle?"

Most of the students were confident that the sum would be 180°, as it was for the block. "I know a concrete way to prove it," I said. I cut out the triangle and tore off each of the corners.

"The reason I tore off corners rather than cut them," I said to the class, "is so I don't get confused about which point was the vertex of the triangle."

I drew a dot on the overhead and placed the vertices of all three angles on it with their sides touching. They lined up to make a straight line. The students seemed impressed.

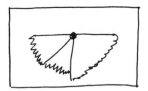

"How does this prove the sum of the interior angles of a triangle is 180°?" I asked.

Several students had responses. "They make a straight line." "They're half a circle." "It's a straight angle."

"What do you think about other-shaped triangles?" I asked. "Suppose I draw a long, skinny triangle. What do you think the sum of the interior angles will be?" No one seemed willing to predict.

"As a group," I said, "investigate the sum of the interior angles of differently shaped triangles. To do this, each of you should draw a triangle on construction paper, cut it out, tear off the corners, and paste them touching a dot as I showed. Paste all your triangles on one sheet of newsprint. Then look at your results and together write at least one statement that summarizes what you notice."

Kristin and Tami verify that the sum of the angles of triangles is 180°.

The groups got to work. Watching the students work reminded me how much students enjoy working with their hands. The summary statements they produced were similar:

"All the triangle corners add up to 180° when put together."

"After you cut out the corners of the triangle and glue them they equal 180°."

"Whatever sizes of triangles you put together they will always measure up to 180°."

As groups finished, I asked them to try the same investigation for quadrilaterals. I told them they were to do this individually. "Each of you needs to do the experiment with four quadrilaterals of different shapes," I instructed. "Make a sketch of each quadrilateral before you cut the corners. After you've pasted down the corners, write a statement that describes what you noticed." Their homework assignment was to complete the quadrilateral investigation. I've found that giving students the chance to get started in class on a homework assignment helps to clarify the directions.

Day 5

"Who would like to read the summary statement you wrote for last night's homework?" I asked the class to begin the lesson.

Tiffany reported first. "I thought they would equal 180° because the triangles did," she said. "But I was proved wrong."

"No matter what angles there are," Leon read, "it always comes out to 360°." Many of the others agreed.

"I noticed that on all the shapes I made a circle going around," Sunnee read.

"That's what I wrote," Jennifer said. Others indicated that they had written something similar.

"I think it's very weird how all corners meet and make a 360° angle," Lori read.

I then wrote "Sum of Interior Angles of Polygons" on an overhead transparency. Underneath I wrote:

$$\text{Triangle (3 sides)} = 180°$$
$$\text{Quadrilateral (4 sides)} = 360°$$

"This is what you know so far," I said. "As a group, investigate the sum of interior angles of other polygons. I suggest you start with the yellow hexagon from the Pattern Blocks since you've already figured the degrees in its angles. Then see if you can use your information to predict the total number of degrees for other polygons. Look for patterns and report what you find."

Some groups had difficulty with this activity. Tearing corners wasn't effective. Using hinged mirrors only helped with some angles. Some students focused on drawing angles that they already knew to find the sums. Others worked from the pattern of the total degrees for triangles, quadrilaterals, and hexagons.

Table 6 made a chart and wrote a conclusion:

3	180	7	900
4	360	8	1080
5	540	9	1260
6	720	10	1440

They wrote: *You keep adding 180° and you get the answers.*

Table 2 wrote: *The sum of the three angles of a triangle equils 180°. There are 3 sides in a triangle. The sum of the four angles of a quadralateral equils 360°. There are 4 sides. The pattern is for each additional side there is another triangle.*

5 sides	3	8 sides	6
6 sides	4	9 sides	7
7 sides	5	10 sides	8

Therefore a decagon with 10 sides would have 8 triangles inside or 8 × 180° which equils 1440°.

Day 6

"How many have used a protractor before?" I asked to begin class. I held up a protractor for the students to see. Most of the students raised their hands, but many commented that they had forgotten or weren't sure about how to use one.

"Tearing corners off triangles and pasting them down told you the sum of the degrees in all the angles," I said. "But it doesn't tell you how many degrees in any one angle. Also, when you were looking for patterns in the sum of interior angles of polygons, I noticed that some of you were frustrated because you had no way to measure some of the angles." Several groups nodded in agreement.

"Help is here," I said. "The protractor is a useful tool for both measuring angles and drawing angles of specific sizes. In a moment, I'll give you each a protractor. In your groups, examine the protractors and talk about how to use one. It may be helpful to use a right angle as a reference since you already know it's 90°."

I distributed protractors, one for each student. The groups immediately began talking about what to do with them. Some were drawing angles and trying to measure them. After a few minutes, I called the class to attention and had them share what they noticed.

"You put the hole on the point," Russell said.

"Yes," I said, "the hole should match with the vertex of the angle."

"The lines of the angle have to be long enough," Alisa said.

"Is it OK to make them longer?" Kristin asked.

"What do you think?" I asked the class.

Richard answered. "It's not how long the lines are," he said, "it's how they open, like the mouth of a shark."

"There are two rows of numbers that are different," Sara said.

"Except the 90 is the same on both," Michelle added.

"Your job," I then said, "is to work with the person next to you and write directions for how to use the protractor. Your directions should tell how to measure angles and also how to draw angles of different sizes. You can include drawings if it will help make your directions clear." I drew an angle on the overhead and labeled the vertex and rays.

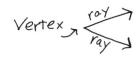

Directions

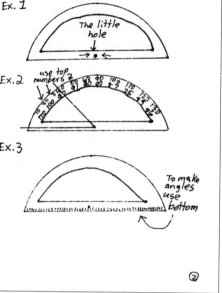

There are 2 things a Protrator does for you it 1. measures angles and 2. It makes an new angles. To measure an angle you put the rough side of the protractor down then put the vertex of the angle in the little hole in the middle, (shown on page 2) and if the angle is acute you use the numbers on the bottom on the right but if it is acute but it is pointing to the left you use the left side and the top. (shown on page 2) To make angles you use the bottom part of the Protractor (shown on Page 2) to make any angle you disire.

①

②

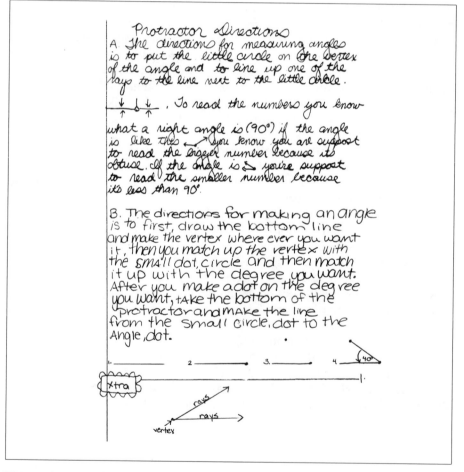

Protractor Directions

A. The directions for measuring angles is to put the little circle on the vertex of the angle and to line up one of the rays to the line next to the little circle.

. To read the numbers you know what a right angle is (90°) if the angle is like this you know you are suppost to read the bigger number because its obtuse. If the angle is you're suppost to read the smaller number because it's less than 90°.

B. The directions for making an angle is to first, draw the bottom line and make the vertex where ever you want it, then you match up the vertex with the small dot, circle and then match it up with the degree you want. After you make a dot on the degree you want, take the bottom of the protractor and make the line from the small circle, dot to the Angle, dot.

Writing directions for using a protractor makes learning about protractors a problem-solving experience.

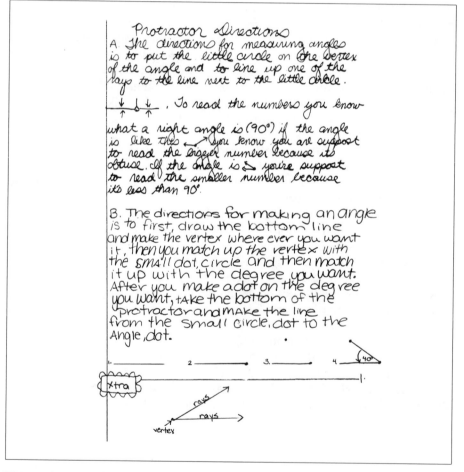

"These words might be useful for you," I said. I also wrote "protractor" and "angle" on the overhead for the students' reference.

"What other words about angles might you use?" I asked. I listed all they volunteered: *acute, right, obtuse, straight, degrees.*

On this assignment, students expressed their thinking in different ways. Jenny and Sara, for example, wrote the following directions for measuring an angle: *First, you make an angle. Then you place the bottom line of the angle on the line of the protractor. Then you put the dot on the vertex of the angle. Then you find out what degree the angle is. If you can't figure it out, you do this. First you find out if your angle is obtuse or acute. If it's obtuse you use the top line, if it's acute you use the bottom line. Then you get the arrow and take it up to the number and the number that the line hits is the degree of your angle.*

Cuong and Cheryl wrote: *One rule you must always remember is you must always have the bulls eye on the straight line at the bottom. If the angle goes to the right you must read the bottom numbers. But if it goes to the left you must read the top numbers.*

Ron M. and Ron S. wrote: *You place the vertex of the angle you are measuring in the middle of the hole. The hole is on the bottom of the protractor. When measuring, let's say that it is 69 degrees. On the protractor it does not say 69°. Only 50, 60, & 70. What you do is measure and count by the lines on top of the protractor.*

Will and Pat designed their work as a pamphlet. They titled it "The Protractor Manual." They wrote: *There are 2 things a Protrator does for you. It 1. measures angles and 2. It makes new angles. To measure an angle you put the rough side of the protractor down then put the vertex of the angle in the little hole in the middle, (shown on page 2) and if the angle is acute you use the numbers on the bottom on the right but if it is acute but it is pointing to the left you use the left side and the top. (shown on page 2) To make angles you use the bottom part of the Protractor (shown on Page 2) to make any angle you disire.*

step 1 - measuring

place the protractor on your paper where the angle is. where you see the vertex put it in the center circle. to find the degrees use the numbers closest to the half circle and there you have it, a measured angle.

step 2 - drawing

after you place the protractor on the paper, place a dot in the center circle. from the dot draw a straight line to right. then look at the degrees closest to the half circle. draw a straight line from the vertex to the degrees. then (hopefully) you drew an angle.

Jenny and Crystal explain how to use the protractor to measure and draw angles.

As they finished, the students exchanged papers and tried others' directions. Reading others' work gave them experience with different viewpoints.

This assignment made figuring out how use a protractor a problem-solving challenge. Working in pairs to write directions resulted in a great deal of discussion about how to measure angles. I think the results were as successful, or even more so, than they would have been had I given the class directions on how to use a protractor and assigned angles to measure. Also, this approach was certainly more interesting and involving for the students.

Final Thoughts

Watching the students work during these activities was convincing testimony about the benefit of concrete materials. Not only did the students thoroughly enjoy exploring with the blocks, mirrors, paper folding and tearing, and protractors, it seemed that the more active their hands were, the more active their minds were. Discussions were animated, and all students were engaged. Classes were a pleasure to watch.

As stated early in the chapter, students had enough previous experience with Pattern Blocks so that they didn't need time for general exploration with them before focusing on the angle activities. However, I allotted time for them to explore with the hinged mirrors.

I've learned from experience the importance of providing time for students to satisfy their curiosity with a material. This time is more than worthwhile—it's essential. It helps lessons go more smoothly and also honors students' needs to become acquainted with a new learning tool.

The emphasis of the angle activities was on the students' actively exploring angles and making sense of a how to use a protractor. The students were in control of their learning. They were the creators of their understanding rather than receivers of explanations from me or from a textbook. Approaching mathematics in this way contributes to helping students see that thinking for themselves is an important aspect of their math learning.

FINDING THE AREA OF A CIRCLE

This unit was developed from an article that appeared in the May 1986 issue of *Arithmetic Teacher*, "Finding the Area of a Circle: Use a Cake Pan and Leave Out the Pi," by Walter Szetela and Douglas T. Owens. The article presents a collection of methods for approximating the area of a circle, a topic usually taught in the middle-school curriculum.

Traditionally, students learn the formula $A = \pi r^2$ and demonstrate mastery by plugging in numbers to get answers. Though teachers may have explained the reason for the formula, it's not unusual for students to calculate areas without knowing why the formula makes sense. As stated in the article, "Unfortunately, numbers, and not understanding, are all that result."

The *Arithmetic Teacher* article offers a different slant. It provides a collection of methods for approximating the area of a circular region. These methods build on methods for measuring the areas of triangles, squares, rectangles, and parallelograms. Though the activities admittedly take more instructional time than merely teaching the formula, they do much more. They promote understanding of the idea of area in general and, more specifically, of the idea of finding the area of circles.

Six of the methods from the article were adapted for this unit. Along with explaining the math explorations, the chapter describes how the explorations were structured into a unit of study and provides details about how the class was organized. Information is included about the materials needed, how the methods were translated into a menu of tasks for the students, how the students' recording was organized, what assessments were done, and how students' work was graded.

The unit was presented to a class of sixth graders and a class of seventh and eighth graders. In both classes, the students worked in pairs. They worked at their own pace and made their own decisions about the sequence in which to do the tasks. The chapter describes in detail what happened in the sixth-grade class and includes a note about some of the differences experienced with the seventh and eighth graders.

Getting Ready

To prepare for the unit, I drew a circle with a radius of 10 centimeters on a piece of paper and duplicated the paper about 60 times. I also drew a 10-centimeter circle on a sheet ruled into square centimeters and duplicated about 30 sheets. This was sufficient for the students to use for all the methods.

By using the same-sized circle to test each of the six methods, the students could compare the approximations of its area that each method produced. Also, because everyone in the class was using the same-sized circle, students could compare their results.

I typed the directions for the six methods to distribute to the students and also prepared a cover sheet of instructions (see p. 112). Even though I planned to introduce the investigations verbally to the class, I know it's helpful for students to have a written reference for clarification.

In addition, I assembled the materials needed. I filled four small plastic bags with lima beans, enough in each to cover the circular region. I bought some pliable linoleum floor covering and cut two circles the same size as the ones I duplicated, six 10-by-10-centimeter squares, ten 10-by-1-centimeter strips, and twenty 1-by-1-centimeter squares. I divided the linoleum pieces equally into two plastic bags. (My local lumberyard sells floor covering in 12-foot rolls. I bought a 1-foot strip, which was about 3 times what I needed. The linoleum was a bargain, as it was on sale for $4.77 a yard.) I set out one pan balance. As for all lessons, rulers, scissors, tape, and calculators were also available for the students.

Discussing Area

I organized students into pairs for the investigation. Before giving them the written instructions and explaining the materials I had assembled, I decided to review what the class had previously studied about area as a way of leading into the new activities.

"What's meant by *area*?" I said, and wrote "area" on the board.

Several students had ideas.

"It's the distance inside something," Chris offered.

"It's the space inside a shape," Meghan added.

"Yeah," Chris blurted out, "it's space, not distance. That's what I meant."

"You do it in square feet," Amir said.

"It has to do with measuring space that's inside a closed figure," Michelle said.

"It's the space inside the perimeter," Nick said.

After all the students who wanted to contribute had spoken, I drew a rectangle on the board. "How would you find the area of this rectangle?" I asked.

"You multiply length times width," Jason and Cory called out, almost simultaneously. Others nodded their assent.

"What does that tell you?" I asked. "Raise your hands if you can explain what multiplying the length by the width tells."

I told the students to raise their hands to discourage them from calling out before being recognized. Also, I wanted to allow time for all students to think about my question. I waited a bit to see which students would decide they could explain this. About a third of the students raised their hands. I called on Meghan.

"It tells you the area," she said. "Like if the length is 8 and the width is 5, then the area is 40."

"How could I show the 8, 5, and 40 on my drawing?" I asked.

Nate answered. "You just draw lines to make squares," he said. "You show 8 squares one way and 5 squares the other."

I divided the rectangle into squares as Nate suggested and said, "Drawing the squares this way may help explain to someone why a rectangle with a length of 8 units and a width of 5 units has an area of 40 square units."

I find that students continually fail to include the labels for units, especially for square units, in spite of my pointing this out repeatedly. I try to draw attention to the correct labels as much as possible, using the correct mathematical language as often as I can.

I drew several other rectangles on the board, including one square, showing how each could be divided into squares to find its area. Then I drew a trapezoid the shape of the red trapezoid from the Pattern Blocks.

"How would you find the area of this trapezoid?" I asked.

After a few moments, two hands went up. I called on Jeff.

"You could draw lines straight down so you have a rectangle in the middle," he suggested. I did this.

 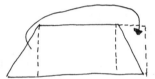

"Oh, I see," Jennifer said. "You could put the triangle from one side on the other so it would be a rectangle. Then it's easy."

I sketched this and commented, "What this does is change a new problem into one you already know how to solve. That's a useful problem-solving strategy and one that works for other shapes as well."

I drew a parallelogram on the board. "Jeff and Jennifer's idea would also work for this parallelogram," I said, illustrating this on the board.

"Other shapes might be more complicated," I said, drawing on the board a right triangle, a hexagon, and an irregular polygon with eight sides. "But you could use what you know about rectangles by cutting and piecing these together to figure their areas."

Matt raised his hand to contribute something he remembered. "The triangle is easy," he said. "You just make it into a rectangle and then cut your answer in half."

From this discussion, I learned that the students knew something about area, though individuals had different bits of information and understanding. Some seemed clear about what area is and how to find it while others were shaky in their knowledge. I wasn't sure about those who didn't volunteer ideas.

Focusing on Circles

I then drew a circle on the board. "What about finding the area inside a circle?" I asked.

FINDING THE AREA OF A CIRCLE

Names _____

This investigation presents six different ways to approximate the
area of a circular region. Following are your jobs for this unit.

1. WHAT TO DO

   Working together as partners, try each method. Make sure you
   agree on your results.

2. HOW TO RECORD

   Getting an approximation is only one part of the goal for each
   method. Also important is to analyze the mathematics of the
   method -- why it makes sense, how accurate it is, and whether
   it's a reasonable approach. Working together, use the following format and write about each method:

   Method No. - Title

   Description: (Tell what you did.)

   Result: (Record your approximation.)

   Analysis: (Describe why the method makes
        mathematical sense. Also describe how
        you feel about the accuracy of the
        method. Include other reactions you
        have.)

   ---

3. REFLECTING ON YOUR EXPERIENCE

   When you and your partner have completed all the methods, individually answer the following questions in writing:

      Which method do you "trust" the most? Why?

4. EXTRA (Optional)

   Invent another method for approximating the area of a circular
   region. Try it. Describe your method and the results.

Note: When you've completed the activities, organize your work
for each method. Make a cover sheet that has a title, date, your
names and include a table of contents for what you're submitting.

FINDING THE AREA OF A CIRCLE

Method 1:   COUNTING SQUARES

1. Using a circle drawn on squared centimeter paper, count all the whole centimeter squares that lie completely inside the circle. (This <u>underestimates</u> the area of the circle.)
2. Now make an <u>overestimate</u> of the area of the circle by taking the number of whole squares that lie inside the circle (the same number you got for step 1) and add to it the number of squares that touch the circle and lie partly inside and partly outside.
3. Average the two counts.

Method 2:   INSCRIBING AND CIRCUMSCRIBING SQUARES

1. Circumscribe a square about the circle. Find its area.
2. Inscribe a square inside the circle. Find its area.
3. Average the two areas.

Method 3:   THE OCTAGONAL (OR EGYPTIAN) METHOD

1. Circumscribe a square about the circle. Find its area.
2. Divide the square into 9 congruent squares.
3. Form an octagon by drawing a diagonal in each corner square as shown.
4. Figure the area of the octagon to approximate the area of the circle.

Method 4:   FINDING THE AREA BY WEIGHING

1. Weigh the circular tile cutout with the rectangular tile pieces.
2. Use the rectangular pieces to approximate the area of the circular region.

Method 5:   THE "CURVY PARALLELOGRAM" METHOD

1. Divide the circle into 8 congruent sectors.
2. Cut out the sectors and arrange them to form a curvy parallelogram.

3. Approximate the area of the curvy parallelogram.

Method 6:   USING BEANS

1. Cover the circular region with one layer of beans. (It's helpful to use a collar to "corral" the beans.)
2. Circumscribe a square about the circle. Cut it into four smaller squares as shown.
3. Rearrange the four squares into a rectangle. Tape the pieces together.

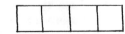

4. Place the beans on the rectangle you've made, pushing them toward one end.
5. Use the area covered by the beans to approximate the area of the circle.

Jennifer suggests drawing a square around the circle to approximate its area.

"You need the formula," Amir volunteered. No one knew or could recall what it was.

"Yes," I answered, "there is a formula. But what could you do to solve the problem of finding the area without a formula?"

Meghan raised her hand. "You could cut it apart and piece it together into a rectangle," she said.

"That would be hard with all the curves," Chris reacted.

"I have an idea," Jennifer said. "Draw a square around the circle." I drew the square.

"Now what?" I asked.

"You can find the area of the square," Jennifer continued. "But that would be too big, so you'd kind of have to figure how much those extra parts were and subtract them."

Some of the others seemed impressed with Jennifer's suggestion. I was impressed also, as Jennifer's idea was close to what the class would do in one of the methods they were going to use.

"Does anyone have another idea?" I asked.

"You could draw a square inside instead," Michael said, "and then figure how much extra you need to add."

I drew a square inside the circle to illustrate Michael's idea. "There are special words that describe the squares that Jennifer and Michael described," I told the class. I wrote "circumscribed" and "inscribed" under "area" on the board.

"Which word describes Jennifer's square, and which describes Michael's?" I asked. It was easy for the class to decide. I then began an explanation of what they would do in this investigation.

"I've drawn the same-sized circle on plain paper and on squared-centimeter paper," I said to the class. I held up a copy of each for them to see.

"In this unit," I continued, "you're going to approximate the area of this circle in six different ways."

"I have another idea," Chris said. "You could count all the whole squares and then figure out how to put the little pieces of squares together to find how many total squares there are."

"That's how I could figure how many squares are in the extra pieces," Jennifer said, referring back to her idea.

"Remember those ideas," I said. "The ones I'm going to describe to you are different from your ideas, but you'll have the chance to try your own method after you've tried the ones I've prepared. Let me explain one method you'll try," I said.

"Should we take notes?" Nell asked, always organized.

"You don't have to," I said. "After I describe a few of the methods, I'll pass out complete instructions, and we'll go over them all together."

I decided to present two methods verbally first, without their having the distraction of looking at papers as well as listening. Then I'd have them read the descriptions to reinforce what I presented and give further directions.

"One bit of useful information," I said, "is that the circle you'll be measuring has a radius of 10 centimeters." I added "radius" to the list of words I'd already started on the board. I wrote "diameter" underneath.

"How long is the diameter?" I asked.

I received a chorus of "20" in reply. Most of them seemed to know the diameter was twice the radius. I drew a circle on the board and labeled the radius and diameter.

"One method you'll use is a combination of what Jennifer and Michael suggested," I said.

I drew a circle on the board and circumscribed a square around it. "First you circumscribe a square as Jennifer did," I said. "Then you figure its area. How would you do that?"

"If the circle were on the yellow paper," Lauren said, "you could count the small squares." The yellow paper was the one on which the circle was drawn over squared centimeters.

"You could measure the length and width and times it," Keky said.

"You just have to measure one side because it's a square," Nell said.

None of the students related the radius or diameter of the circle to the side of the square. I showed on the board that the side of the square was equal to the diameter, but I know that students only use methods that they understand and are comfortable with.

"The area of the circumscribed square overestimates the area inside the circle," I said. "Who can explain what I mean by that?"

This seemed obvious to the class. About a third of the students raised their hands. Josh explained.

"That's the first part of this method, getting an approximation that's too big," I continued. "Then you inscribe a square, as Michael suggested, and figure that area, which will be too small an estimate. The final part of the method tells you to come up with an approximation between these two areas by averaging."

There was a chorus of murmurs from the class: "Oh, that's neat." "I get it." "Nifty."

Though I wasn't sure they all understood averaging, I decided to have them face that with their partners and ask me later if needed.

"The method I just explained is number 2 on the sheet I'll pass out in a moment," I said. "Method number 1 also has you average but in another way."

I held up a circle on the squared-centimeter paper.

"In this method, you again overestimate and underestimate and average the two," I explained. "To underestimate, you make a count of all the whole squares that lie inside the circle. To overestimate, you make a count of all the squares inside or touching the circle, whether or not they're whole squares. In this second count, some of the squares you include are on the circle, with part inside and part outside. Then you average these two counts."

I continued now with instructions for how I expected them to record. "For each of the six methods you try," I said, "you and your partner are to make a record using a separate sheet of paper for each method. There are four parts to what you write on each sheet: title, description, result, and analysis."

I drew on the board a facsimile of a sheet of paper and showed how I wanted it structured. I gave further directions. "Copy the method number and title from your sheet of directions," I said. "For the description, tell what you did. Then record the approximation you got. Be sure to label your answer." I wrote "square centimeters," "sq cm," and "cm²" on the board to give them options for labeling their answers.

"The analysis is the part of your recording," I continued, "where you describe why the method makes mathematical sense and how you feel about the accuracy of the method. Also, you can include any other reactions or thoughts you have in this section."

I added one comment before passing out the written directions. "You need to have one record sheet for each method for the two of you," I said, "and I'd like you to discuss your ideas before either of you begins to write."

Then I passed out the two direction sheets, which I had stapled (see illustrations). "Put your names on the first sheet. Together, read what I've written before I give you more information."

I gave them time to look over what I had prepared. I realized that this was a lot of information for them to absorb, but I've learned from experience that it's worth the effort to give directions as completely as possible before students plunge into work. After they had had time to read the material, I called them back to attention.

"I'd like to talk a bit more about the other methods," I said, "and show you the materials you'll be using. I've described the first two. For number 3, use the circle on the plain paper. It might be helpful to make a note of this on your instructions." I waited for them to do this.

"Again, circumscribe a square about the circle," I continued. "Then divide this square into nine congruent squares, and draw diagonals as shown to form an octagon." I added "congruent," "diagonal," and "octagon" to the list on the board and had students explain each.

"Then you figure the area of the octagon and use that as an approximation of the area of the circle," I said.

"How do we do that?" Amir asked.

"I won't answer that just now," I responded. "Try and figure it out when you get to it. I'll help if you and your partner are stuck."

"For number 4," I continued, "you'll need to use one of the plastic bags of linoleum pieces and the pan balance. Weigh the circular tile, which is the same size as the circle on the paper, with the rectangular pieces. Use the information you get to approximate the area of the circular region."

There were no questions. I knew they were anxious for me to stop talking so they could get started. But I pursued the directions for the last two methods.

"For method 5," I said, "make a note to use a circle on plain paper. Cut out the circle and then cut it into eight sectors as if you were cutting a pizza. Arrange the eight sectors to make a 'curvy parallelogram,' as I drew." I added "sector" to the list of words.

"What's a *curvy parallelogram*?" Keky asked.

"It looks like a parallelogram," I said, "but the two long sides aren't straight. They're pieces of the circumference."

"How do we find its area?" Keky pursued.

"I know," Michael said, "you do length times width like with the other parallelograms."

"These are the things you'll need to discuss with your partner when you work," I said.

"One more method," I continued. "Take a plastic bag of beans for this and cover a circle, patting the beans carefully into one layer."

"Which circle do we use?" Nell asked.

"Either will do," I said. "It's up to you and your partner to decide. Then draw a circumscribed square, cut it into fourths, tape the squares into a rectangle, and rearrange the beans to see how much of the rectangle they cover. Use this to approximate the area of the circle."

I gave a few last directions before letting them get to work. "You can try the methods in any order you like," I said. "Decide with your partner which you're interested in trying first. Only one pair can do method 4 at a time, though, since we only have one pan balance. Any questions?"

There were none. At this time, only fifteen minutes remained in the period, and they all began work. I circulated, answering questions. "Which circle should we use for method 1?" "Can we work on separate ones?" "Do we each have to record?" "Which is an easy one?" "I don't get number 5." "What do I write?"

I answered their questions as briefly as possible, encouraging them to work through their initial confusion with their partners. I planned to talk with the whole class at the beginning of the next period about some of the questions they raised, but wanted them to all have some beginning experience. Their confusion was typical for the beginning of a unit such as this. I've come to learn that students settle down once they feel more comfortable with what they're expected to do.

Beginning the Second Day

Before having the students begin working on the second day, I talked with them first. I wanted both to answer the questions they had and to bring attention to some issues of concern to me.

"Before you get back to work on the circle activities," I said, "let me have your attention for a few minutes." The students were in various stages of getting settled and organized for work.

"What do I do?" Melissa asked. She had been absent the day before.

"Me, too," Gabe said.

I settled the class down. "Who can describe for Melissa and Gabe what you began working on yesterday?" I asked.

"We have these circles," Cory said, "and we have to figure out their area in a bunch of different ways. Each of the ways is on this sheet." Cory held up her sheet of instructions for Melissa and Gabe.

"Does anyone have anything else to add?" I asked.

Keky raised her hand. "You use the yellow sheet for some and the white sheet for others depending on whether you'll need the little squares or not." She held up a sample of each and continued, "Like for the one with counting squares you have to have the squares, but you don't need them for all the others."

"You get your answers in square centimeters," Michael added, "and you can write that three different ways. See up there on the board?" Michael pointed to where I had written "square centimeters," "sq cm," and "cm²."

"All the answers are approximations," Chris said.

It was interesting for me to hear what the students had to offer in their descriptions. It gave me feedback on how they had interpreted the directions I had given.

"Can Gabe work with us?" Jeff asked.

"No, Melissa and Gabe can be partners together," I said. I had them move so they were seated together. "I'll help you get started once the class gets to work," I told them.

"I want to talk a little bit about the writing I've asked you to do for each method," I then said to the class. "I read a book last summer titled *Writing to Learn* written by William Zinsser. The book gave me a great deal to think about, and one quote from the book has stuck in my mind: 'Writing is how we think our way into a subject and make it our own.' "

I repeated the quote for the class (Zinsser 1988, 16) and then asked, "What do you think Mr. Zinsser meant when he wrote that?"

Several of the students had ideas to share.

"When you write something down in your own words, then you really understand it," Chris said.

"Your own words belong to you," Keky said, "and they're your ideas and no one can change them."

"You have to think about something before you can explain what you think in writing," Meghan said.

"When you have to write something," Nate said, "then you have to organize your thoughts. You can't just write something down; you have to think it through."

"I don't know how to say this," Amir began, "but when you have to write, first you have to figure out what you're going to write or else you can't write it."

"Writing forces you to think," Michael said.

"All of your ideas explain how writing is a way for you to get your thinking down on paper," I said after all the students who raised their hands had had a chance to speak. "You expressed your thoughts in your own words. Writing down those thoughts would be a way to think even further. I believe that having you write encourages you to think more fully about the mathematics you are doing."

I then continued with another reason for writing. "Not only does writing help you think about the mathematics you're exploring," I said, "but it helps me as a teacher, too. When we have a class discussion, not everyone gets the chance to say what they think. But it's important for me to know what each of you is thinking and to learn as much as possible about what you're learning and understanding. Your writing gives me insights into each of your ideas. So I'd like the recording you do to be as thorough and thoughtful as you can make it."

Meghan raised her hand. "Sometimes I don't know what to write."

"Writing is an extension of your thinking," I answered. "Sometimes it's easier to say your ideas than write them. That's where partners can help each other. Discuss what you think with each other to help you form your ideas into words you can write down. If you're both stuck, then raise your hands, and I'll help you start discussing what you've done."

"Is it OK if we divide the work so we do different methods?" Gabe asked.

"It's all right to share the work," I answered. "But what's important is that you each understand each method well enough so you could explain it to someone else. Also, even though only one of you will do the actual writing for a method, I want you first to discuss together what you're going to write. Explore your ideas together and then write as detailed a report as possible to help me understand your thinking."

"What do you do if you get different answers?" Keky asked.

"You most likely will get different answers for the different methods because they're all approximations," I answered.

"That's not what I meant," Keky went on. "Suppose you and your partner both do the same method and get different answers."

"That could happen as well," I said. "Try and identify why they're different. You may be able to come to an agreement on one answer or you may need to report both results in your record."

This was a good time to have them begin working. "Continue where you left off yesterday," I said. "Remember, you can do the methods in any order you like, but be sure to take special care with the write-ups."

Annette raised her hand. "Jennifer's absent," she said. "What should I do?"

I called Annette, Melissa, and Gabe to the front of the room. First I answered Annette. "Continue working by yourself," I said. "Then when Jennifer returns, you'll need to explain to her all that you've done."

Annette nodded and returned to her seat.

Then I went through an introduction of the methods for Melissa and Gabe. Rather than go through all six methods, I explained just the first one and told them to complete it and then call me over for further instructions. This gave me the chance to get back to supervising the rest of the class.

Observing and Helping Students

Students worked in different ways. Some pairs worked together on each method. Some tackled different ones. While some wrote descriptions after doing each method, others preferred to do all the methods first and the writing later.

When students asked me for help or reassurance that they were on the right track, my first response was to see if partners had checked with each other. If not, I would have them talk with each other and call me back if they were still stuck. If partners both had the same question, I would listen to what they had done so far and then give them feedback.

"We don't know what to do with the octagon," Jeff reported for him and Chris.

"What have you done so far?" I asked.

"We drew the square and divided it into 9 squares," Chris showed me. "Then we drew the lines to make an octagon."

"Now what?" I asked.

"We don't know," Jeff said.

"The method is based on the assumption," I explained, "that the octagon is pretty close in area to the circle." The boys nodded.

"You divided the circumscribed square into 9 squares," I continued. "How many of those 9 squares are taken up by the octagon?"

"Five," Jeff said.

"Yeah, but look," Chris added, "there are extra pieces. That's 5½, 6, 6½, 7. It's 7. Is that it?"

"I agree with that," I said, "but you'll have to convince Jeff as well."

"But then what?" Chris said.

"If you knew what the area of one of the small squares was," I said, "then you could find the area of the octagon."

"I get it now," Chris said.

"Explain what you understand to Jeff," I said. "I'll come back in a bit and check on how you're doing."

That seemed to be enough for the boys. When I checked back in a few minutes, I noticed they were using a ruler to measure the side of the smaller squares. As they were busily at work, I didn't interrupt them.

Meghan called me over. She and Cory had weighed the linoleum pieces and gotten an answer of 310 square centimeters. They were writing their report.

"I think this method works," she said, "because the square pieces really are the same amount as the circle, but they're just in different shapes."

"Yes," I answered. "What you describe makes sense to me, and that's just the kind of explanation you need to make in the analysis."

"Can we use a drawing?" Cory asked.

"Yes, that would be fine," I said. "Include whatever will help make your explanation clear."

Sometimes I'd notice students were on the wrong track. For example, Katie and Jason made an error with the first method. They counted the number of whole squares inside the circle and got an underestimate of 282. Then they counted just the squares touching the circle, getting a count of 58, instead of the overestimate they were supposed to figure, which included the first count as well. Their averaging produced an answer of 170.

"Something doesn't make sense here," I said to them. "What does 282 tell you?"

"It's how many squares are inside the circle," Jason answered.

"Is that number greater or less than the area of the circle?" I asked.

"Less," they both answered.

"Yes, it's an underestimate," I said. "But your final answer of 170 is even smaller. That doesn't make sense." I pointed to their work.

"Uh oh," Katie said, "we must have counted wrong."

"We couldn't have," Jason said, "we checked."

The students use different methods to approximate the area of the circle.

I reminded them about averaging an underestimate and overestimate to get an approximation of the area. "You didn't make an overestimate. An overestimate would include all the squares inside the circle, that you already counted, as well as the squares touching the circle. That would be 282 plus 58."

That was enough for them and they got back to work to revise their answer.

A few other pairs of students ran into the same problem. Rather than go through the explanation with them, I had them go and ask Jason and Katie for help. Explaining would help Jason and Katie cement their thinking. Also, it would keep me free to help others.

At this moment, Michelle and Gabe had completed the first methods and needed further directions. Also, Amir and Michael were stuck on the octagonal method. I had Amir and Michael get help from Chris and Jeff and went to talk with Michelle and Gabe.

There was a great deal of activity in the room. I was busy helping and directing. The class still didn't seem settled in the project, as students were still struggling with the unfamiliarity of what they had to do. But the students' activity seemed generally purposeful.

When talking with students, I continually reminded them that their job was to do what made mathematical sense to them. Getting right answers quickly to finish wasn't the goal; rather, investigating different mathematical ways to approach finding the area was most important. I also prodded them to describe fully what they did. Getting students to focus thoughtfully on their tasks and write clear and thorough explanations takes the time and effort of consistent reinforcement.

When only about four minutes remained in the period, I asked the students to get ready to leave. "Collect your work," I said, "and keep it together so you're ready to begin work when you come to class tomorrow.

The Next Few Days

When students arrived the third day, I had them get right to work. I wanted to institute the procedure that when they came to class, they were to get started immediately on their investigations. With periods only forty-three minutes long, it's important to make good use of all the time available.

Students became more self-sufficient in their work over the next few days. Partners devised their own systems for working. There was interaction among pairs as they checked with each other for advice.

While the students worked, I circulated. I answered questions, directed students who seemed to be wandering to get back to their task, observed what pairs were doing, and listened to students' discussions. This kind of setting in the classroom is enormously valuable for informally gathering information about what students do and think. It allows for observing and interacting with students in ways not possible during whole class lessons when the teacher is presenting information or leading a discussion.

It was interesting for me to notice the different approaches students used. For example, when students were trying the octagonal method, some measured the sides of the small squares as Chris and Jeff did. Their results differed depending on the accuracy of their drawing and measuring.

Other students, however, had different approaches. Marissa wrote the following for herself and Lauren: *I multiplied 20 × 20 to get the area of the square. I got 400. Then I divided 9 into 400 because there were 9 squares and by doing this I got the area of each square. Next I multiplied 7 × 44. I did this because 44 square centimeters are in each square and there are 7 squares in the octagon.* They had done their calculations with pencil and paper.

Bryan and Jon used the same method as Marissa and Lauren did but didn't round off. They had used a calculator. Jon explained how he drew the octagon and then continued to write: *I found how many littler squares there were, and I got seven. I found the area of one of them by dividing 400 by nine and I got 44.$\overline{44}$. then I took 44.$\overline{44}$ and multiplyed it by seven.* When results were presented the next week, Bryan explained that the line above the 4s indicated that it kept repeating. This was new notation for most of the students and a nice way for it to be introduced.

Michelle and Gabe used a different procedure. Gabe wrote: *We found the area of the octagon by finding the area of the whole big square and subtracting the part that wasn't also part of the octagon.* They had multiplied 44.44 by 2 and subtracted that from 400.

Cory and Meghan arrived at their result by multiplying 400 by 7/9. Cory explained: *The reason why I × 400 by 7/9 is because there are 9 squares alltogether and seven of them are in the octagon.*

When working on method 1, most students did what Nell and Keky described, although they arrived at different numerical counts: *We counted the squares that were completely inside the circle and got 284. We then counted the squres that had any bit of the circle inside them and got 344. We added 344 and 284 and divided by two to get our answer.*

Michael and Amir, however, used a shortcut. They wrote: *First, we counted the whole centimeter squares that lie completely in the circle. To make sure that we didn't lose our count we numbered inside the squares. After we had numbered half-way through the circle, we figured out that all we had to do was double the last number instead of numbering the rest of the circle.*

It took most of the students about five class periods to do all six methods and write their descriptions. Then they had to write individual reactions, describing the method they "trusted" the most and explaining why. Finally, they had to make a table of contents and organize and assemble their work into a booklet.

Organizing their work is a way to have students take another look at what they've done. Too often, when students finish their work, they never take a second look at it. They're no longer interested in examining what they did. Having them prepare what they've completed to submit encourages them to review their work.

Because some students always work more quickly than others, it's a good idea to have an extra optional activity. Though the students had the option of inventing another method for approximating the area inside the circle, none of them was interested in this. They were given another option on the fourth day. It was an activity called Half the Circumference. Using the circle they had been measuring as a basis, students were to draw a circle with a circumference half as long, approximate its area, and draw a conclusion about the relationship between the areas of the two circles. Three pairs of students did this task.

Reading and Evaluating the Students' Work

I read each of the students' booklets twice. My first reading gave me an overall sense of their responses. As I read through them, I made a chart of the approximations they reported.

Method	1	2	3	4	5	6
Josh and Jon	309	298	294	308	305	308
Bryan and Jon	305	310	311.11	312	310	320
Nell and Keky	313	298	316	306	303	missing
Michelle and Gabe	311	298	308	311	310	307
Lauren and Marissa	265.5	291	308	312	310	300
Jennifer and Annette	316	$49\,in^2$	312	312	$48\,in^2$	306
Chris and Jeff	310	312.5	304	311	310	311
Katie and Jason	312	305.5	410.8	312	300	316
Meghan and Cory	305	300	312	310	305	300
Amir and Michael	313	300	308	311	$36\,in^2$	311
Graham and Jason	319	298	310.8	306	384	¾ of the rectangle

Even though I had observed the students working during class, I was surprised by what I read in some of their reports. For example, two pairs of students measured in inches for some of the methods, making comparison with centimeters difficult. Three pairs either neglected to include units in their reports or used incorrect labels. There was a missing task in one folder and missing individual reactions in two. One pair didn't write any analyses for their methods. They realized this, too late, and wrote an "Oops, sorry" apology.

There were differences in the contents of their reports in clarity, thoroughness, and mathematical insights. The greatest variation in quality occurred in what they included in their analyses.

Some of the students' analyses gave insights into their mathematical thinking. For example, one student gave the following explanation for the octagonal method: *I think this was a good method because the octagon is almost the same size as the circle so it gives almost acurate results.* Another student wrote: *This makes mathematical sense because if you look at the octagon and the circle the space they both occupie is incredibly similar.*

In contrast, other analyses expressed a minimum of mathematical interpretation. For the same method, a student wrote: *I feel that this answer is pretty accurate because I had to go through a lot of multiplying and adding ect. to get the answer.* Another wrote: *This method is good. It is accurate and takes only a short time. I would recommend it.*

Some of their writing revealed a struggle in their thinking. Also for the octagonal method, a boy wrote: *The only reason that this method works is that the octogon is shaped remotely like the circle. I don't feel that this method is very acurate because the shape of the octogon is too "squarey" to be acurate. Except for the fact that I tried this method, I wouldn't have thought that it would work. I really don't know why. It just*

Jason and Katie clearly explained why method 1 made mathematical sense to them.

Method #2

Inscribing and *Circumscribing* Squares

First we circumscribed a square about the circle and found it's area. It was 400 square centimeters. Then we inscribed a square around the circle and found it's area. It was 211 square centimeters. Then we averaged the two areas. The answer we got was 305.5 square centimeters.

This method sort of makes mathematical sense because when you circumscribe and inscribe the circle or square (whatever) you take some off then add it back on.

Brian and John weren't quite sure why method 2 made sense.

looks like the octogon is much too small. But I was wrong. (When I questioned what he meant by "this method works," he said that the answer he got was close to his other approximations.)

There was a similar range in the responses for other methods. For the analysis about the method that involved using beans, one student wrote: *It seemed to be a very odd method. The beans were fairly hard to work with, but I managed!* Another student wrote: *This experiment works because the area is shown by the same size units. By filling the circle with beans and using the same amount on a different figure, the area of beans will always equal the same area no matter what the shape is.*

I've come to expect such differences in the students' work. I know that students come to class with varying backgrounds of experience and different understandings. Partial understanding and confusion are natural aspects of the learning process. The more insights I have into students' thinking, the more able I am to make instructional choices that can add to their growing knowledge.

When reading the reports for a second time, I responded to each in writing. I planned to return the reports with my comments and give the students the opportunity to improve upon their work before I gave final grades. I feel that written feedback lets the students know that I have read and thought about their work. It helps them learn more about my expectations and standards. Also, when they read my comments, students have another chance to reflect on what they've done. Though grading is necessary, I'm interested in keeping the focus on their exploring and thinking as much as possible. The following are samples of what I wrote for several students.

Bryan and Jon "The descriptions you wrote for the six methods were clear. However, when you gave your reactions to each method, you didn't include very much about your *reasons*. It's your thinking that I'm interested in.

> *Method #3—The Octagonal Method*
>
> Description—I first made a circumscribed
> circle and then filled in the square
> with an octagon. After I did that I
> saw than five hole squares and
> four halfs of a square. Then I saw
> that each square was 44.4 cm
> and so I just multiplied and got
> the answer.
> Results— 310.8 cm — approximation
> Analysis—I feel that this answer
> is pretty accurate because I had
> to go through a lot of multiplying
> and adding ect. to get the answer.
> It makes sense because all squares
> equal the number of centimeters multiplied
> by number of square.

Jason and Graham were satisfied that the multiplying and adding they did insured the accuracy of their answer.

"Look at the reactions you each wrote for Counting Squares, for example. Bryan, you wrote that it was a good estimate but you didn't think it was effective. Why wasn't it effective? And Jon, you said you thought it was one of the more accurate methods. Why did you think that? Please rethink your reactions and add to what you've already written.

"Also, there are a few things missing:

1. Table of Contents
2. An individual paper from each of you that answers the following: Which method do you 'trust' the most? Why?

"P.S. I enjoyed your cover drawing."

Nell and Keky   "Most of the descriptions you wrote for each of the six methods were clear, and your unit was presented well. I have some questions, however, about some of your work. I'd like you to consider and respond to my questions. You can write your responses on a separate sheet of paper or add them to the appropriate sheets in your folder.

Method #4 - Finding the Area by weighing

You had to take 1 lindum circle, 3 squares, 5 1/10 squares and 15 1/100 of 1/10 squares. You had a scale - ⊏◫⊐ and you had to put the circle in one cup, and tried to equal the weight of the circle by using 3 squares, 1/10 squares. 1/10 of 1/10 squares.

Result 3 10³cm

You had to take the shapes, square, 1/10, 1/100 of 1/10 and equal a circle. If you took an exacto knife and cut all the shapes, you could make the perfect replica for example!

circle

peices

Meghan and Cory illustrated their reasoning about method number 4.

"Method 1: You said the method got you close to the initial answer. What do you mean by 'initial answer'? Please explain.

"Method 3: This method did not call for averaging. It called for figuring out the area inside the octagon by using the 9 smaller squares you drew. Try to do this and explain the answer you get.

"Method 5: How did you figure out the area of the curvy parallelogram? Please explain.

"Still missing from your project are the following:

1. Method 6
2. Your individual reactions. This is to be an individual paper from each of you that answers the following: Which method do you 'trust' the most? Why?"

Amir and Michael "I enjoyed reading your work. What you wrote was descriptive and gave me good information about your thinking.

"Notice that for method 5, you measured in inches rather than in centimeters. This makes it difficult to compare the answer with the other methods. Please change your answer."

Method #5 The Curvy Paralelogram method

Description: I used the white paper and cut out the circle. Then I folded it so it had eight sections. I cut out all eight sections and made a paraletogram out of them, like this:

— then, I meavsured the parrelogram and found the approximate area of it.
Results: The area of the parrelogram was 310. So, the circle will be around 310.
Analysis: I furd that this was a very good method, but it might not be right because the parrelogram was very curvy and so the meavsurments might be a little messed up. I have gotten three answers that are practically the same though, 308, 310 (this one), and 312 (the wieghts).

Melissa and Lauren's analysis revealed their skepticism about method 5.

Summarizing the Unit with the Class

To begin a class discussion, I wrote on the board the students' results for the first method. I didn't include the students' names because I wanted them to focus on the mathematics, not on who got which answers.

Method 1

309	310
305	312
313	305
311	313
265.5	319
316	

Method #6   Using Beans

Description: I started off by filling in the circle with beans. Then, I cut the circle into four smaller square pieces. I organized the pieces into a rectangle and taped them together. I then began to fill in as many of the squares as I could with the beans. 3 of the squares were covered completely. I still had a few left over beans.

Result: The result is pretty much an educated estimate. The beans had covered 3 of the 4 portions of the rectangle. Since each of the small squares equal 100 of the 1 centimeter^2 boxes, 300 of the centimeter squares were covered. Yet, the extra beans were also lined up on another row. Our estimated guess seems to be very close to being exact. We got 311 approximately covered centimeter squares.

Analysis: At first, I was very confused. But when I went over the instructions again, it was all very clear. It seemed to be a very odd method. The beans were fairly hard to work with, but I managed!

Michael and Amir seemed satisfied with their effort for method 6.

"What do you think about the range of results?" I asked.

"They're pretty close," Michael said.

"Except for the one that's under 300," Nate added.

"Maybe they counted wrong," Keky said.

I posed another question. "How come there are different answers when you all used the same circle on the same squared-centimeter paper?" I asked.

"Well, it was hard to tell if some squares were really touching or not," Melissa said, "so some people could have included some that others didn't."

"They're just approximations," Cory said.

"You could make a mistake counting," Chris said. "There's a lot of counting."

"What ideas do you have about why the method called for taking the average of the two counts?" I then asked.

"You add them and then divide by 2," Keky said.

"I agree that that's how to find the average," I said, "but what does finding the average tell?"

Too often, students learn how to do a procedure without learning what the procedure accomplishes or why it makes sense. I waited to give the students time to think about my question. Not many volunteered to respond.

"It gives you a better answer," Lauren said.

"When you average, you get something in between," Amir said.

"Yeah," Chris added, "your answer is bigger than the first and smaller than the second."

"Because the first is too small and the second is too much," Nell said. "The average is about right."

I gave all the students who had an idea the chance to speak and then posed another question.

"Do you think this was a good method for finding the area?" I asked.

"I think counting all the squares made it very accurate," Jessica said.

"It was neat," Jason said. "I like the way it worked."

"It was too hard," Jeff said. "There was too much counting."

"Michael and Amir used a shortcut for counting," I said. "Could one of you describe what you did?"

Michael volunteered. He explained, "We only counted squares for half the circle and multiplied by 2." There were some murmurs of respect for his explanation.

I then changed the focus to the second method of circumscribing and inscribing squares.

"Let's take a look at the approximations you got for the next method," I said. I wrote these results on the board.

Method 1	Method 2
309	298
305	310
313	298
311	298
265.5	291
316	49 in^2
310	312.5
312	305.5
305	300
313	300
319	298

"There are more answers the same," Graham said.

"Why do you think so?" I asked.

"I know," Chris blurted out. "It's because we all measured the same-size squares, and that was easier than doing all the counting."

"What's that 49 mean?" Keky asked.

"That one was measured in square inches, not square centimeters," I explained. "You'll be getting your folders back with my comments, and you'll have the chance to make changes. The answer may be sensible, but measuring in square inches makes it difficult to compare with square centimeters."

I continued in this way with each method, having students share their reactions and posing questions to have them reflect on the mathematics. As I posted the results for each method, the students broke out into chatter among themselves. They were interested in the information. They were willing to contribute to the class discussion and were animated in doing so.

After discussing their experiences and approximations for the "curvy parallelogram" method, I said to the class, "I'm going to give a short explanation about the curvy parallelogram method that has helped others understand the formula for finding the area inside a circle: $\pi\, r^2$."

When I had their attention, I continued. "You may not understand my explanation," I said. "That's OK, because you'll get a chance to hear it again in math classes, maybe next year and the year after. But see if you can make sense of this now."

I know that teaching by telling doesn't always work and that following someone else's reasoning is difficult. But I decided to take this opportunity to offer an explanation to the students and give them the opportunity to consider the mathematics behind the formula.

I drew the curvy parallelogram on the board. "Instead of measuring the base and height of the parallelogram as you did," I said, "I'm going to think about those measurements differently. First of all, the height of the parallelogram is equal to the radius of the circle. Who can explain how I know that?"

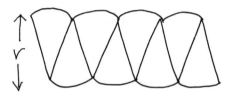

Jason came to the board and drew a radius on one of the sectors to show what I meant.

"The base of the parallelogram," I continued, "is equal to half the circumference. Who can explain that?"

"Because it has four of the eight curvy parts," Meghan said.

"Half is on the top and half is on the bottom," Chris added.

"Remember that the circumference is equal to pi times the diameter," I said. I wrote on the board:

$$c = \pi\, d.$$

We had investigated that relationship earlier in the year. The students had measured the diameters and circumferences of many circular objects I had brought to class—jar lids of various sizes, a Frisbee, several phonograph records, coasters, paper and plastic plates, plastic cups and bottles, a mirror, a lampshade, a wastepaper basket. The students recorded their measurements on a chart on the chalkboard. I then had the class look at the chart and see what relationships they could find between the diameter and circumference measurements. Calculators were particularly useful for them to verify that the circumference of each circle was approximately 3 times the diameter. In this way, I introduced the idea of pi as a number that was an approximation of 3.

"Since the radius is half the diameter, then half the circumference is pi times the radius," I said. I labeled the base of the parallelogram $\pi\, r$.

"So if I multiply the base times the height," I concluded, "that is $\pi\, r$ times r, which is the same as $\pi\, r^2$."

Jason draws a radius on one sector to show it's the height of the curvy parallelogram.

I estimated that about a third of the students followed this explanation. I reassured the class about my purpose in telling them this.

"Don't worry if this doesn't make complete sense," I said. "You'll have other opportunities to learn about this as you study math. If you don't understand this now, you may be able to the next time you encounter it."

Students were interested in seeing their work and my comments. Before I returned their folders, however, I wanted to talk a bit more and give them an additional writing assignment. I was interested to see how their thinking and writing might be different after our class discussion.

"Before I return your work," I said, "I'm interested in whether you would recommend this unit for other classes?"

Their reactions were positive.

"I liked the activities," Amir said, "especially the weighing and using beans. I liked to draw too."

"I think it was interesting to learn different ways to find the area," Lauren said. "I think that would be good for other classes."

"It's a good break from book work," Jeff said.

"It made you think and it was fun," Jason said.

"It was a lot of work," Cory said, "but it kept you involved."

I then said, "I'm also interested in your ideas about what mathematics you think you learned from these activities. For homework, I'd like you to write about what you think these activities helped you learn."

"How much should we write?" Gabe asked.

"At least a page," I said. I find that setting a minimum length provides a useful parameter for students.

An assignment such as this is a useful way to assess what the unit accomplished. Despite our best teaching efforts, the *taught* curriculum and the *experienced* curriculum are not always the same. Having students write is a way to understand their individual perceptions of the learning experience better and to gain insights into their mathematical understandings.

Michael wrote: *This was a good asignment because it expanded our minds to find different ways to find the area of a circle instead of doing the old mathematical way. The ways we did the methods were wierd. I never thought we could do it. But doing this porject is good comunication. We did it with partners so we learned to work together and learn the new methods.*

I learned about that if you shuffle pieces around you could make an easier object to find the area. Like in the curvy parallelagram method we shuffled the pieces around to make an easier object.

Cory wrote: *I really never knew their was so many ways to find out the area of a circle. I learned about circumscribing, inscribing, weighing a circle made out of linoleum, how to find the area with beans, centimeters squared, and how it has to do with a circle, averaging numbers, counting squares and then averaging those numbers together, and experimenting with all these things.*

> Math
>
> Circle
>
> What I learned From This
>
> Me and Jeff were partners on an experiment to Find the area of circle, We were given six methods to experiment with,
>
> After we completed the experiment I thought that the experiment really did teach me a lot.
>
> One thing was that there is <u>always</u> more than one method in finding the answer in mathmatics.
>
> That was proven by the six different methods to Find the circles area.
>
> I also learned that finding the area of a circle isn't impossible (even though that is what I thought before).
>
> I learned the methods themselves for Finding the area of a circle,

Chris gave his perspective on what he learned from this unit.

What I Learned

I learned a lot of ways to find the area of a circle. I was especially amazed that you could find the area of a circle by weighing. I mean that nobody would think of finding an area by weighting, they would rather think of multipling or something more mathematical.

I learned that you can take something apart and put it back together in a different shape and that could help you find the area of something (like the curvy parellogram method). The same area can be found if you take something apart and put it back together in a different shape.

"What I Learned"

What I learned from this project was how to work better with people and get along with them better. I also learned how to find the area of a circle in a couple of fun and exciting ways. Such as weighing, counting, etc.. I really don't know when I'll have to use this skill, but I guess its a good skill to have.

Having students write about their experiences is a way to compare the *taught* curriculum and the *perceived* curriculum.

I'm sure that everybody has written this. "I have learned what the area of a circle is which is $\pi \times r^2$." But a teacher just didn't say it when he/she was in the front of the class. They proved *it and thats one of the things that makes this project so special.*

Jason wrote: *What I learned from this project was how to work better with people and get along with them better. I also learned how to find the area of a circle in a couple of fun and exciting ways. Such as weighing, counting, etc. I really don't know when I'll have to use this skill, but I guess its a good skill to have.*

From Lauren: *I learned a lot of ways to find the area of a circle. I was especially amazed that you could find the area of a circle by weighing. I mean that nobody would think of finding an area by weighing, they would rather think of multipling or something more mathematical.*

I learned that you can take something apart and put it back together in a different shape and that could help you find the area of something (like the curvy parellogram method). The same area can be found if you take something apart and put it back together in a different shape.

A Note about a Class of Seventh and Eighth Graders

The unit had a different flavor in a grades seven and eight pre-algebra class. Most of these students knew the formula for finding the area of the circle and quickly figured that the area of the circle was 314 square centimeters. Their focus was to see how close to this answer the approximations were for each of the methods.

I handled the summarizing discussion the same way as I did with the sixth graders. These students' responses, however, reflected their extra year or two of experience with mathematics.

For an assessment at the end of the unit, I gave the students a homework assignment to see how they might apply their understanding of area in another problem situation.

"I'd like you to investigate the prices of different-sized pizzas and see how these prices relate to their areas," I said. I gave them specific directions orally.

"What you're to do," I said, "is to phone a pizza place and find out how big each size pizza is and how much it costs. Then figure whether the prices make mathematical sense with regard to their sizes, whether the prices are proportional to the sizes of the pizzas. If they do make sense, explain why. If not, tell what you would charge and why."

"Does it matter which kind of pizza we ask about?" Jon asked.

"No," I replied, "as long as you use the same kind of pizza for each price."

"Do we have to figure their areas?" Brent asked.

"I don't want to give you hints for this," I said. "I'm interested in how you'll go about solving this without my help."

"Could you say the problem again?" Jenny asked.

I repeated the problem.

"Do you have it written down?" Mike said. The class was accustomed to getting their assignments in writing.

"No, I haven't written it down," I said. "Would you each take out a sheet of paper now and write the problem down in your own words?"

In this way, I took the opportunity to give them experience with formulating the problem in their own ways. I gave them time to do this and then had several students read what they had written.

Amanda wrote: *Call up a pizza place and ask the size of each of their pizzas—small, medium, and large. Then ask the prices. See if the prices are proportional to the areas of the pizzas. If they are not, reprice them.*

Brent wrote: *For this problem we are supposed to determine whether the price of pizza is proportional to the different sizes you can order.*

Allison wrote: *Call or visit a pizza place. Find out the size and price of pizzas. Then decide whether it's mathematically sensible or not. How much would you charge?*

Jennifer wrote: *What we are supposed to do is to call or visit a pizza place and find out what the price of each pizza is and what size it is. We then have to decide whether or not the prices are acceptable. If they aren't, what would we change them to?*

Geoff wrote: *What are the prices of a small, medium, and large pizza? Do they make mathematical sense? If so, why? If not, what should they charge?*

Most of the students figured the area of each pizza in square inches and then figured how much a square inch of pizza costs for each size. In most cases, the larger pizzas were less expensive per square inch. Some students decided the prices were close enough and were fine. Others presented alternative pricing. Their solutions and explanations gave me information about what they understood, not only about the area of circles, but about other mathematical ideas as well.

Final Thoughts

I saw a sign while traveling in Colorado that read: "Hindsight is always 20-20 vision." In that light, an idea occurred to me about another way to assess students' understanding about area. After completing this unit, I'd like students to consider an irregular bloblike shape and decide which of the methods they used to approximate the area of the circle would be appropriate for the blob. I'd ask them to explain why the ones they identified made sense and why the others wouldn't. I'd also ask them to choose the method they think would be "best" for approximating the area and to explain why.

I'm interested in starting the unit another time by having students first try their own ways to approximate the area of a circle before I introduce them to the methods suggested in the *Arithmetic Teacher* article. I'd like students to understand that mathematical ideas and methods are invented by people engaged in looking for relationships and connections.

I was pleased with the unit and look forward to presenting it again to students. Along with contributing to students' understanding about finding the area of circles, the unit encouraged students to communicate about mathematical ideas. It gave them experience with using data to judge the effectiveness of mathematical methods. Also, it gave them a mathematical experience that involved them with several areas of the curriculum: number, geometry, measurement, and logical reasoning.

LESSONS ON PERCENTS

Students have many experiences with percents before they study them formally in school. They know that a 50 percent sale means that prices are cut in half and that a 10 percent sale doesn't give as much saving. They understand what it means to earn a 90 percent grade on a test. They hear on TV that some tires have 40 percent more wearing power, that a tennis player gets 64 percent of her first serves in, that there is a 70 percent chance of rain tomorrow. Common to these sorts of experiences is that percents are presented in the contexts of situations that occur in students' daily lives.

The goal for instruction in this unit was to help students learn to use percents appropriately and effectively in problem situations. That means that when given a situation that involves percents, students would be able to reason mathematically to arrive at an answer, be able to explain why that answer is reasonable, and make a decision about the situation based on the answer.

It makes sense that formal lessons on percents build both on what students already know and how they gained their understanding. Instructional activities should expand students' knowledge from their daily life experiences into more general understandings. They should help students relate new situations with percents to situations already familiar to them.

Implementing this approach required first gathering a sizable collection of activities. Key to these activities is that they focus on students' thinking and provide the opportunity for students to create their own understandings of how to reason with percents. Also, to help students see mathematics as a study of interrelated ideas, activities should use ideas from different strands of the math curriculum. In this selection, the investigations draw from the areas of geometry, measurement, and statistics.

Deciding which activities to introduce and in what sequence called for making judgments. There was no recipe to follow. It's important to note that the order in which the activities are presented in this section is not meant to suggest an essential instructional sequence, or hierarchy of experiences. Structuring an instructional sequence requires learning about what students do and do not understand and about what sorts of activities and topics interest and motivate them. To this end, a good deal of class time was devoted to having students talk and write in order to collect information about them. Students were given many opportunities for whole class and small group discussions to verbalize their ideas, their methods, their confusions, and their understandings. Also, they wrote often, which helped them reflect on their learning as well as provided information about their thinking.

The lessons in this chapter do not describe all that was actually offered to the students to help them learn about percents. However, the lessons included represent the kind of instruction provided throughout the entire unit and offer sample ways to introduce ideas about percents, suggest problem situations that engage students, and give alternative methods for assessing what students understand.

Videotape "Sense or Nonsense?" and "What Percent Is Shaded?" on Part 3 of *Mathematics for Middle School* show the actual lessons that are described in this chapter.

Introducing Percents—Sense or Nonsense?

The Sense or Nonsense? activity, which appears in *Problem Solving in Mathematics: Grade 7* from the Lane County Mathematics Project (Scaaf et al. 1983), works well to begin a unit on percents. Not only does the activity introduce students to what they'll be studying, but it also initiates discussions that provide a way to assess the students' current understandings.

To prepare for the lesson, I duplicated enough Sense or Nonsense worksheets to have one for each group. As for all their lessons, the students were seated in groups of four. They were accustomed to working cooperatively.

I wrote Sense or Nonsense? on the board and gave the following directions to the class. "The activity we'll do today will give me a better idea of what you understand about percent," I began. "Take a single sheet of binder paper for your group, put each of your names on it, and title it 'Sense or Nonsense?'"

I gave the groups time to do this. I've found that when students get organized before I introduce a task, they're more settled during the lesson, their thoughts seem clearer, and the quality of their written work is better.

I showed the students the worksheets. "There are 10 statements on this worksheet," I told the students. "Listen as I read number 1: 'Mr. Bragg says he is right 100 percent of the time.' Do you think Mr. Bragg is bragging? Why?" There were some giggles and side comments from the students.

"Discuss this in your groups," I then said. "Decide whether you agree or disagree and be prepared to explain why." My plan was to have the groups work independently and write responses for each of the 10 statements on the worksheet, but I felt that a class discussion of the first one would help to clarify the task.

The students readily offered their thoughts about Mr. Bragg. "We think he's bragging, because no one can be right all of the time," Armand reported for his group.

"He can't be right every single time because what about the things he doesn't know?" Danelle reported.

"He's not right," Darshana said. "No one is perfect."

"Nobody's perfect, and 100 percent of the time means always," Tamika said.

SENSE OR NONSENSE

Decide whether these statements are reasonable.
Explain why or why not.

1. Mr. Bragg says he is right 100% of the time.
   Do you think Mr. Bragg is bragging? Why?

2. The Todd family ate out last Saturday. The bill was $36.
   Would a 50% tip be too much to leave? Why?

3. Joe loaned Jeff one dollar. He said the interest would be 75%
   a day.
   Is this a pretty good deal for Joe? Why?

4. Cindy spends 100% of her allowance on candy.
   Do you think this is sensible? Why?

5. The "Never Miss" basketball team made 10% of the baskets they
   tried.
   Do you think they should change their name? Why?

6. Sarah missed 10 problems on the science test.
   Do you think her percent is high enough for her to earn an A?
   Why?

7. Rosa has a paper route. She gets to keep 25% of whatever she
   collects.
   Do you think this is a good deal? Why?

8. The weather reporter said, "There's a 100% chance of rain for
   tomorrow."
   Is this a reasonable prediction for this month? Why?

9. Ms. Green was complaining. "Prices have gone up at least 200%
   this past year," she said.
   Do you think she is exaggerating? Why?

10. A store advertised "Best Sale Ever, 10% discount on all
    items."
    Is this a good sale? Why?

Sense or Nonsense

① Yes, _we agree_ because nobody's perfect and 100% of the time means always.

② Yes its too much because, 50% is half so half of $36 is $18.

③ Our group does not think its a good deal because 75% of $1 is 75¢. In two days, Jeff would already owe more than Joe had loaned him.

④ Our group does not think Cindy should spend 100%, or all of her allowance on candy.

⑤ We agree that the team should change their name. If they only make 10% of the baskets, they are missing more than half the time.

⑥ Our group thinks Sarah's score on the test depends on the number of problems on the test.

⑦ Our group thinks 25% is not enough money for Rosa to be collecting on her paper route.

⑧ Our group believes the forecaster's prediction is reasonable because in winter it rains a lot.

⑨ We agree Ms. Green was exaggerating because the most that prices could go up would be 100%

⑩ Our group does not believe this is the "Best Sale Ever" because everything's only 10% off, which is less than half.

Students worked in groups of four to discuss and explain their responses to the "Sense or Nonsense" statements.

Sense or Non-sense

1. yes, he is bragging because no ones perfect.

2. yes, because regular tip us 15% *it is too much*

3. No, it is not a good deal for Jeff because, it would be 75¢ a day which is more than 50%

4. No, it is not sensible to spend 100% on candy because then you don't have any money left and you don't need that much candy.

5. yes, they should change their name because they only make 1 basket out of every 10 shots.

6. not enough info because if there was 100 problems she might have gotten an A but if there were 20 she would have gotten an F

7. yes, because all she has to do is roll them up and deliver them.

8. No, it isn't a reasonable prediction because it is allmost Spring and the weather man couldn't be 100% sure

9. yes, she is exaggerating because all the prices would triple

10. No, it is not a good sale because it depends on the price of the clothes

Sense or Nonsense

1) Mr. Bragg is bragging because nobody's perfect and also some questions don't have a right or wrong answer.

2) A 50% tip would be too much because 50% means half and half would 18 dollars. So 18 dollars plus $36 equals $54 and that's too much money.

3) It'll be a pretty good deal for Joe because he only loaned Jeff a dollar and Jeff would have to at least 75¢ more than he borrowed.

4) Cindy spending 100% on candy is not sensible because that's all her money.

5) Yes, they should change their name because "Never miss" means that they never miss and they only make one out of every ten.

6) Doesn't make sense because we don't know how many problems were on the test.

7) Rosa is not getting a good deal because that's only 25¢ per dollar, newspapers only cost 25¢ and she also has to labor and it takes part of her time.

8) It's reasonable because it just rained yesterday.

9) Ms. Green is exaggerating because that's three times as much as the regular price.

10) It's not a good sale because if something costed a dollar before the sale, then you would only get 10¢ off.

<u>Sense</u> or <u>Nonsense</u>

1. We think Mr. Bragg is bragging because no one is right 100% of the time

2. 50% is too much of a tip to leave because that would be another 18 dollars on top of the 36 for the meal. 15 to 20% would be reasonable

3. This is a good deal for Joe because he makes another 75 cents along with his dollar per day that Jeff doesn't pay him back

4. We don't think this is sensible because then Cindy has no money for anything else.

5. We think the "Never Miss" basketball team should change their name because to never miss you have to shoot 100% not 10%

6. We think this <u>could</u> be possible to get an A. It depends how many problems were on the science test

7. We think this deal is okay. We think Rosa should get a little more than 25% because she has to wrap the papers, and deliver the papers by herself.

8. This isn't a reasonable prediction for a month because some areas on Earth are subject to sudden, drastic weather changes.

9. We think Ms. Green is exaggerating because inflation these days is ridiculous but not that ridiculous.

10. This is not a good sale because 10% is only 1/10 off the regular price.

"We think he's bragging," Dan reported, "because nobody's perfect and if he is always right, then he would be like Albert Einstein."

"He has to be bragging," Renae said. "Nobody's perfect, and also some questions don't have a right or wrong answer."

Their responses indicated to me that the students grasped the idea of 100 percent. (For students who didn't know, I counted on the small group discussions and the whole class reporting to help them develop understanding.)

I then gave the class further instructions. "I'm going to give each group a worksheet of the Sense or Nonsense? statements," I said. "Have someone in your group read a statement and then talk about whether it's reasonable or not, making sure everyone in your group has a chance to express his or her ideas. Have one person record what you decide. Since you've already discussed the first statement, begin by having someone write your group's explanation of why you think Mr. Bragg was bragging."

The groups' discussions were active. As I circulated, I noticed that the most heated discussions were about number 6: "Sarah missed 10 problems on the science test. Do you think her percent is high enough for her to earn an A? Why?" Many of the students were clear that you would have to know how many problems were on the test, which indicated to me that they understood that a percent isn't a number but describes a relationship between quantities. Others argued for different positions. Nin, Jon, and Lemuel, for example, felt that she would get an A because 90 percent is an A−.

As usual, some groups finished the worksheet more quickly than others. I asked them to have someone read aloud to the group what they had written to make sure their work accurately represented their thinking. The period seemed to go quickly, and there was no time for processing their group work as a whole class. I collected their papers just before the bell rang.

I began class the next day by returning the papers to the groups. "Take a few minutes to review your work," I said, "and choose one of your explanations to read to the class." I didn't give any guidance about which to choose. My feeling was that explanations for any of the statements could spark discussion. Also, I was interested in hearing which statements they would pick.

One group was particularly proud of their explanation for number 8: "The weather reporter said, 'There's a 100 percent chance of rain for tomorrow.' Is this a reasonable prediction for this month? Why?"

Laura reported what her group had written. "No," she read, "because it depends on how fast the wind will carry the clouds through during the night."

Several groups chose to report on number 6: "Rosa has a paper route. She gets to keep 25 percent of whatever she collects. Do you think this is a good deal? Why?"

Sunhee read, "Rosa is not getting a good deal because that's only $.25 per $1.00. Newspapers only cost $.25, and she also has labor and it takes part of her time."

Craig reported, "No, because she did all the work."

"No, it's a rip-off," Joey reported, "because she only gets one-fourth back and say she gets $100.00, she would only get $25.00, and that's not enough."

Responses from other groups revealed that most of the students agreed. Gina, for example, said her group felt Rosa should get 50 percent. Paula, however, reported that her group thought that Rosa was paid enough. "All she has to do is roll them up and deliver them," she said. (I chose not to discuss the economic realities of being in the work force, but in retrospect, this would appear to be a good way to integrate math with social studies.)

After each group had a chance to report one of their explanations, I asked the class about number 6, Sarah and the science test. I was interested in their ideas about how many problems would have to be on the test for Sarah to miss 10 and still earn an A. It was hard to get their enthusiasm up for this discussion, so I didn't push it. There would be plenty of other opportunities for me to pose questions of this type to the class, and it didn't seem vital to press for a response right now. It was clearly my interest and not theirs. Instead, I posed something different for them to consider.

"I have another statement for you to think about," I said. "For this one, I'd like you to think silently about it for a few minutes, then discuss it with the others in your group, then each write in your notebook what you think." It's valuable at times to have students write individually so that those who don't volunteer to do so in their groups have writing experience as well.

I then told them the statement. "The weather forecaster said there was a 60 percent chance of rain on Saturday and a 40 percent chance of rain on Sunday," I said. "Therefore, there is a 100 percent chance of rain on the weekend. Does this make sense?"

After they had all written in their notebooks, I began a class discussion. Nathan spoke first with great confidence. "This has got to be false," he said, "because you don't add the percents, you average them."

Kim was huffy about the stupidity of the question. "They are different days, so you can't add them," she said.

Teddy tried to explain why it didn't make sense to add them. He said, "60 percent on Saturday means *not* 100 percent on Saturday. 40 percent on Sunday means *not* 100 percent on Sunday. You can't have a 100 percent chance unless it is 100 percent on both days."

Two groups felt it was reasonable to assume that there was a 100 percent chance of rain on the weekend. They were unable, however, to explain why they thought so. All Kiet could offer was, "60 percent plus 40 percent equals 100 percent."

It was now the end of the period, and I left this discussion unresolved. I used to feel that it was important to bring lessons to some conclusion by the end of a period. I've come to realize that too often I was responding to my need for closure, a need that was neither necessary nor appropriate for the students, and I was focusing more on my teaching than on the students' learning. I'm now more comfortable letting an idea hang for several days, even longer, knowing that time and additional experience can be useful for taking a later look.

One value of this two-day lesson for me was in my ability to gain beginning understandings of what ideas about percent were clear and fuzzy to which students. For the students, the activity was an opportunity to think about percents in real world contexts. Also, they had the chance to talk about their ideas about percents with each other. I felt it was a good beginning.

(*Note*: The next day Kiet had changed his position from the one he had offered in the class discussion. "If a weatherman says there is a 60 percent rain on Saturday and a 40 percent rain on Sunday," he explained to me, "then we wouldn't have a 100 percent chance of rain over the weekend because if we have a 100 percent rain in the weekend, then why say both 60 percent on Saturday and 40 percent on Sunday?")

A Geometry Perspective—What Percent Is Shaded?

This second activity from the Lane County Mathematics Project materials (Scaaf et al. 1983) presents percents from a different point of view. What Percent Is Shaded? uses a spatial model. Students are given squares with different-sized and -shaped regions shaded. They make estimates about what percent of each square is shaded. The activity introduces students to the idea that percents are parts of 100 and also gives them experience with the idea of area.

To prepare for the lesson, I duplicated for each student a What Percent Is Shaded? worksheet and a transparent 100-Grid. The grids were the same size as the squares on the worksheet. I began the lesson by drawing a square on an overhead transparency. I drew an irregular shape inside the square and shaded it in.

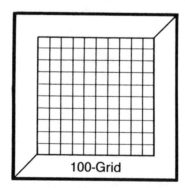

"About what percent of this square do you think is shaded?" I asked. "Write your estimate in your notebook." I purposely drew an irregular shape that couldn't be easily or exactly calculated. I was interested in posing a problem for which there could be some variation in reasonable responses, not one that called for an exact answer that could be clearly proved right or wrong.

There was a wide range in the estimates students reported. I didn't tell the correct answer or comment on individuals' responses; rather, I asked them to explain how they got their estimates and used their responses to add to my on-going assessment of their understandings.

Then I showed the class one of the transparent 100-Grids I had prepared.

100-Grid

"This grid is the same size as the square on the overhead," I said. I placed the grid over the square to demonstrate this.

"The grid is divided into 100 smaller squares," I continued. "How can this help you make an estimate of what percent of the square is shaded?"

"You could count and see how many little squares are in what you shaded," Morton said. There were murmurs of agreement.

"What would that number tell you?" I asked.

"How much is shaded," Susan said.

"But my question was 'What percent is shaded?,' not 'How many squares are shaded?,' " I responded. "How could the grid help you decide what percent is

The class is asked to figure out how much of the square is shaded.

shaded? Talk about this in your groups." Giving students a chance to talk among themselves is a way for more of them to express their ideas. It also helps them gather their thoughts before presenting them to the class.

I brought the class back to attention and called on Paula. "How many small squares are shaded tells you the percent," she said, "because there are 100 small squares altogether, and percent is part of 100."

"Does anyone have another way to explain that?" I said.

Loc volunteered. "There are 100 small squares," he said, "so 1 of them is 1 percent, and 2 is 2 percent, and 50 is 50 percent. So whatever number of squares you get, that's the percent."

With that introduction, I showed the students the worksheet I had dupli-cated with 9 squares, part of each shaded in. "I'm going to give each of you a worksheet and a transparent grid," I said. "To begin, you are to work individu-ally. For each square, first estimate how much of the area is shaded and then use the grid to measure. When you've all done this, compare your answers in your group. If there are differences, work together to agree on an answer that makes sense to all of you."

The students got right to work. Their involvement indicated to me that the activity was interesting to them. It took the students about fifteen minutes to complete the worksheet and compare their answers. Then, as a class, we dis-cussed some of the tricky ones: numbers 5, 8, and 9. For number 8, I had several students demonstrate on the overhead how they arrived at their answers.

WHAT PERCENT IS SHADED?

Estimate the percent shaded in each square. Discuss your estimates in your group and then use a transparent 100-grid to check them.

1.

Estimate _____

Answer _____

2.

Estimate _____

Answer _____

3.

Estimate _____

Answer _____

4.

Estimate _____

Answer _____

5.

Estimate _____

Answer _____

6.

Estimate _____

Answer _____

7.

Estimate _____

Answer _____

8.

Estimate _____

Answer _____

9.

Estimate _____

Answer _____

It was interesting to note which students seemed to feel more comfortable and confident with this spatial activity than with the Sense or Nonsense statements. I think that providing different approaches to an idea such as percents gives students a variety of options for developing understanding.

Mental Calculation with Percents

This lesson describes how I tried to build on students' understanding of percents to focus on calculating with percents. This activity also comes from the Lane County Mathematics Project materials. It introduces a way for mentally figuring percents of numbers. I taught the lesson not with the goal of having students learn and follow my exact procedure but with the purpose of presenting one option to them for finding percents of numbers. My focus was on having the students make sense of a method that they might find useful, rather than on their learning a particular procedure.

To prepare for the lesson, I wrote the following on an overhead transparency:

50% of $200 is _____ .

25% of $200 is _____ .

10% of $200 is _____ .

5% of $200 is _____ .

1% of $200 is _____ .

Before turning on the overhead projector, I orally presented some questions to the class. "What is 50 percent of $100?" I asked. Most of the students' hands shot up to answer this.

"Raise your hand if you can explain how you know the answer to this question," I asked. Though a few students looked a bit hesitant and lowered their hands, most kept their hands raised. I feel that whenever students are asked for answers, they should also be expected to explain how they got them and why they make sense. When asked to explain their thinking, students learn that it's their thinking that's being valued, not merely being right.

I called on Percy. "It's $50," he said.

"Explain that, please," I said.

"It's easy," Percy said. "50 percent is half, and half of $100 is $50." There were many nods.

"Here's another question," I said. "How much is 25 percent of $100?" Again, many hands went up. I called on Audrey.

"It's $25," she said, "because 25 percent is half of 50 percent, and half of $50 is $25." Again, there were many nods.

"Did anyone figure this a different way?" I asked.

Phi raised his hand. "I just divided $100 four ways and got $25," he said.

"I don't get it," Kim said.

"It's like four quarters in a dollar, but bigger," Phi added. "There are four $25s in $100." Kim nodded, but I wasn't convinced she followed Phi's reasoning.

I then raised a new question. "What about 10 percent of $100?" I asked. This time, fewer hands were raised.

"Before I call on anyone to respond," I said, "discuss this in your group." I gave them a moment to do so, and then called them back to attention.

"Who now feels they could explain how to find 10 percent of $100?" I asked. More hands were raised. I called on Nin.

"That's one-tenth," he said, "so one-tenth of $100 is $10."

I continued with 5 percent of $100 and 1 percent of $100. There were some students in the class who hadn't volunteered to respond to any of the questions. Some students are reticent to speak out in class because of shyness. Others lack confidence in their understanding of the subject matter. I find that having the students work in small groups serves to involve more of the students in discussions. It gives them a chance to talk and encourages their participation. I believe that talking about ideas contributes to students' learning. It allows them to frame their thoughts and communicate them to others, to compare ideas and offer each other reactions. It gives students other perspectives on their own thinking. I now moved the lesson into small group work.

"You'll now get the chance to try some percent problems with your groups," I said and turned on the overhead projector so they could see the chart I had made. "One person in your group needs to copy the chart from the overhead. Then fill it out together, discussing how you arrive at each answer. Be prepared to explain to the class your reasoning for each one."

The groups did this fairly quickly. I had groups report the methods they used to the class. There were variations in their thinking. For example, when explaining how he figured that 25 percent of $200 was $50, Craig said, "You double it."

"What did you double?" I asked Craig.

He responded. "Since 25 percent of $100 is $25," he said, "and since 200 is twice 100, $50 should be twice of $25."

Kim had another way to explain it. She said, "If 50 percent of 200 is $100, so 25 percent is half of 50 percent, so half of $100 is $50."

Gary volunteered another explanation. He said, "If I double the percent, the first number, then I come up with the answer."

"Why does that work?" I asked.

"First I divided 200 by 2 and I came up with 100, and I kept doubling," Gary answered.

Nathan offered another method. "I just got the answer because 200 divided by 4 is $50," he said.

Frank had yet a different way. "I split 200 into 2 hundreds," he said, "and 25 percent of 100 is 25, and 25 percent of the other 100 is 25, so 25 plus 25 is $50."

I feel that having students invent their own strategies for calculating mentally with percents helps them develop tools for finding percents in ways that make sense to them. Also, class discussions provide opportunity for students to hear a variety of ways to think about percents.

With this introduction to different ways to calculate percents, I gave the class the homework assignment of making a similar chart for other numbers: $500, $1600, and $180. To extend this, students would combine the amounts on their charts to figure other percents.

A Statistical Investigation—The School Bus Problem

This lesson presents a problem that involves thinking about percents and left-handed students. The lesson demonstrates one way to integrate topics in math, this time, statistics and number. Also raised in the lesson was the issue of whether to teach algorithms.

The students indicate on a graph whether they are left-handed or right-handed.

I often have students respond on graphs when they enter class. At the beginning of the year, I have each student make a small magnetic tag with his or her name on it. I do this by cutting index cards into tags about ¼ by ¾ inches, using a different color for each of my five classes. I back each tag with a magnet cut from a strip of magnetic tape, the kind that's used on refrigerator doors. (The tape is available in ¼-inch width with a sticky back. You can find where to buy it by checking in the yellow pages under "Magnetic Supplies.") When the students respond to a graph, I can easily see who is absent.

To begin class on this day, I had the students indicate on a graph whether they were right-handed or left-handed. Of the 23 students in the class, 2 indicated that they were left-handed. After a discussion about ambidextrous people, I asked the students to discuss in their groups what percent of the class was left-handed. "Agree on a reasonable estimate," I said, "and be able to explain how you got it."

Most of the groups used the same approach to figure that about 9 percent of the class was left-handed. Teddy explained for his group: "Since 23 is close to 25," he said, "I figured that each person would stand for about 4 percent since 25 goes into 100 four times. 4 times 2 people is 8 percent, but it would be a little more than 8 percent because 23 is less than 25, and each person should stand for a little more."

I then told them that according to a book I read, *The "Average American" Book* (Tarshis 1979), from 12 to 12½ percent of Americans are left-handed. This prompted a discussion about the accuracy of the book, how the authors might have arrived at that figure, and how the statistic might compare to our school population.

I then posed a problem to the class. The problem was created by Lynne Alper, a mathematics educator with the EQUALS program at the Lawrence Hall of Science in Berkeley, Calif. "A school has 500 students," I said. "If a school bus holds 75 students, is there enough room on one bus for all the school's left-handed students?" I had the students work with partners. I asked them to solve the problem and explain in writing how they arrived at their answers.

As I circulated, I noticed that several pairs of students multiplied in order to find out if there was enough room on the bus. Liz and Audrey, for example, wrote: *To get the answer we multiplied 500 students by 12% and got 60 people and the bus can hold 75 people so there is enough room.*

Joey and Tony multiplied 12.5 times 5 and got 62.5. They rounded this up to 63 and wrote: *Yes, because there are 63 students that are left handed.*

Other students used different reasoning processes. Marshay and Kiet wrote: *Yes, there are enough seats to hold all of the left-handed people because 10% of 500 is 50 people, 2% of 500 is 10 people, so 50 plus 10 is 60 people, and each bus holds 75 people.*

Eric and James wrote: *Yes, there are enough seats on the bus to fit the left-handed children. There are 63 left handed kids. We got the answer by using part of our homework. 10% of 500 is 50. 5% of 500 is 25—this was halved.*

Khalil and Gina took a completely different approach. They wrote: *We think you can because 75 is 15% of 500. We only have to put 12% on of the left handed people.*

Some groups used division. Jon and Phi divided 12 into 500 and wrote: *After we did the problem we got 41.66 and it kept on going on so we rounded it off to 42 students. We then subtracted 75 into 42 and got 33. After we got 33 seats we knew all the left handed people could get on the bus.*

Raymond, Paula, and Stephanie also used division, but they divided 500 into 12. They wrote: *Yes, 12 ÷ 500 = 0.024 (12% ÷ 500 students) so out of 500 students 24 of them are left handed so the bus can hold all the left handed people.*

Tamika and Shannon called me over for help. "We're stuck," Tamika told me. "We can't decide whether to divide 12.5 into 500 or 500 into 12.5." She and Shannon had done both divisions and didn't know what to do with either answer.

I called the class back to attention to discuss what they had done and see if I could learn more about their thinking. I wasn't sure where to begin. It seemed to me that students used one of two basic approaches. While some took a "reason it through" approach and traced some line of logic, others were at a loss and went for a "just do something" approach. Even with their differences in methods and understandings, there was full consensus that the left-handed students could fit on the bus.

I began the class discussion by asking for someone to explain what his or her pair had done. Jimmy volunteered and reported that he and Ed had decided that there was enough room by multiplying 500 by 12 percent to find that there were 60 left-handed people.

"Why did you multiply?" I asked.

Jimmy answered, "Because we tried everything else, and it didn't work." The class laughed. Neither Jimmy nor Ed could explain what they meant by "it didn't work."

"Did anyone else multiply?" I asked. Several students raised their hands.

Yes, there are enough seats to hold all of the left handed people because 10% of 500 is 50 people, 2% of 500 is 10 people, so 50+10 is 60 people and each bus holds 75 people.

We think you can because 75 @ is 15% of 500. We only have to put 12% on of the left handed people

There will be 60 left-handed students on the bus.

Out of 100 12% would be 12 people. Since 500 is 5x more than 100 you times

$12 \times 5 = 60.$

Students solved the school bus problem in a variety of ways.

"Can anyone explain why multiplying makes sense?" I asked.

Audrey raised her hand. "Doesn't 'of' mean 'times'?" she said.

"Say a little more about what you're thinking," I probed.

"Well," she continued, "we wanted to find out what was 12 percent of 500, and I remembered that *of* means 'times'. So we multiplied." Audrey shrugged, unable to offer any further elaboration.

Still rummaging for how to process this experience, I directed attention to another method used by some students. I asked Jon and Phi to tell the class what they had done. Phi explained that they had divided 500 by 12 to find there were 42 left-handed students.

"Why did you divide?" I asked them.

Jon answered. "Because it was the first thing that came into our minds."

I asked if anyone could explain why either multiplying or dividing made sense in this situation. There was silence. Finally Dwight raised his hand.

"I thought the same as Audrey," he said. "When it says *of*, you should multiply."

"Did you multiply?" I asked.

"No, well sort of," he said. "Should I read how we did it?"

"Yes, let's hear," I answered.

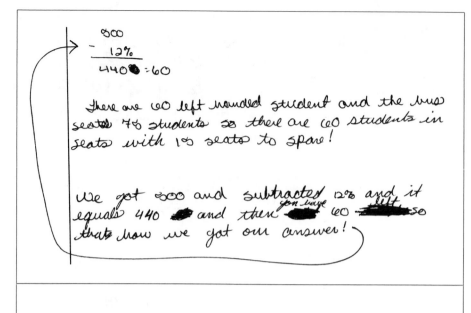

800
- 12%
440% =60

there are 60 left handed student and the bus
seats 78 students so there are 60 students in
seats with 18 seats to spare!

We got 800 and subtracted 12% and it
equals 440 ~~son haye~~ and then ~~~~ 60 ~~left~~ so
~~that~~ how we got our answer!

yes,
12 ÷ 500 = 0.024 (12% ÷ 500 students)
so out of 500 students 24
of them are left handed so
the bus can hold all the left
handed people

It's important to have students explain their thinking. Sometimes right answers hide
a lack of understanding.

Dwight read, "We got the answer by taking 10.0 percent of 500, which is 50.
Then we took 20 percent, which is 10. Then we took 2 people for the half because 12.5 percent could fit."

"That's kind of how we did it," Eric said. "James and I did it like our homework last night."

Jon raised his hand. "Well, which way is right?" he asked.

This brought me up against one of the dilemmas of teaching. Too often, students are very willing to solve a problem with a method that makes no sense to
them, eager to just get the work done. This reminded me of a quote from W. W.
Sawyer, a British mathematician:

> The depressing thing about arithmetic badly taught is that it destroys a child's intel-
> lect and, to some extent, his integrity. Before they are taught arithmetic, children will
> not give their assent to utter nonsense; afterwards they will. Instead of looking at
> things and thinking about them, they will make wild guesses in the hopes of pleasing
> a teacher.

It's disturbing that students are so ready to guess what might be right or what
the teacher wants instead of thinking the problem through and making choices
based on what makes sense to them. This amounts to a trading away of their
own beliefs and integrity to please authority. Is this what we teach in math-

ematics? Does mathematics instruction, in its traditional form, contribute to the intellectual deadening of learners?

In one way, it seemed that Jon's question now presented me the opportunity to "teach" the students that if they multiplied 500 by 12 percent or 12.5 percent, they'd know about how many left-handed students there were. Multiplying works in this situation, but how does telling the students that multiplying is appropriate help them learn when it makes sense to multiply in percent problems? How will they know when multiplying is correct in other situations? How will they learn to recognize situations that call for dividing instead of multiplying?

One of the reasons I choose not to focus lessons on teaching the methods for three kinds of percent problems typically presented in textbooks is that I've found that the students then focus on the algorithms rather than making sense of situations. Students become concerned with "What do I do to get the answer to this problem?" rather than "How can I reason out this situation?"

Teachers often fear that if they don't teach the standard procedures for percent problems, students won't be able to "do" these types of problems. My fear, on the other hand, is just the reverse. I worry that focusing on the standard procedures for percent problems will result in students' not being prepared to reason with percents in order to solve problems.

I struggled how to answer Jon's question so that I would be consistent with my goal of encouraging students to learn to reason for themselves. (Thinking and teaching at the same time is difficult.) In situations such as this one, I try to offer an explanation to students with a light touch. That means I don't want to withhold my knowledge, but I don't want to impose it. I know that my thinking may or may not further their understanding or help them think about the immediate situation. I'd like my explanation to offer them *a* way to approach the problem, one that makes sense to me, not *the* way they must follow.

If my explanation makes sense to them, that's fine. But if my method doesn't make sense to them, I do not want them to mindlessly follow it to please me or get the work done. I want them to know that what's important to me is their thinking, their reasoning, and their understanding.

"Let me tell you how I thought about the problem," I finally said in response to Jon. "I approached it as you did on the work in class yesterday and on last night's homework. I figured that 10 percent of 500 is 50 students, because 50 is one-tenth of 500. Then I figured that 1 percent is 5 more students. I added 50 and 5 and 5 and got 60 for 12 percent. I didn't bother with the extra half percent. I decided that if the school fits the national statistics, even with some small difference, the left-handed students should fit on the bus."

Some students were nodding; others looked blank. "How many of you were able to follow my reasoning?" I asked. About half raised their hands.

"It turns out," I continued, "that I get the same answer of about 60 students if I multiply 500 by 12 percent. Multiplying is appropriate. But when you use a method, you must be able to explain why that method is appropriate."

"So dividing is wrong?" Jon asked.

"The answers some of you got from dividing, that there were 42 or 24 left-handed students, don't make sense," I answered. "Because I know that 50 students is 10 percent, I know that neither 42 students nor 24 students can be 12 percent. That these wrong answers led to the correct conclusion that the left-handed students would fit on the bus was a coincidence." Jon's shoulders sank.

"Don't worry about being confused," I said. "I don't expect you to understand percents completely now. That's why we're studying them. I have more lessons planned to help you learn."

I added one last comment. "What's important," I said, "is for each of you to learn to deal with percents in ways that make sense to you and that you can explain to someone else. We'll keep working at this in class."

This experience illustrates a danger of an answer-oriented emphasis in assessment. Correct answers can hide ignorance. All the students would have gotten this problem right on a traditional multiple-choice standardized test. Yet the judgments we might make on the basis of such correct responses run the risk of being way off. Just as likely, also, is that wrong answers can mask true understanding. In either case, it's important that the emphasis in both teaching and assessing be on students' thinking and reasoning processes, not merely on their abilities to arrive at correct answers.

Percents in a Social Situation—Figuring Tips

This lesson presents problem situations about tipping in restaurants, another contextual setting that involves percents. Students' experiences with eating meals and tipping in restaurants differ, and this lesson also presents the opportunity for a discussion about social conventions.

It's generally thought that 15 percent is an acceptable and appropriate base to use when deciding how much tip to leave. There was a time, not too many years ago, when a 10 percent tip was adequate. I've sometimes wondered how the convention came to be changed and how the change became common knowledge and practice. I haven't wondered very much about this, however, and merely have gone along with the social custom of 15 percent.

Many students approach mathematical procedures in just this way, as if they are social customs to be learned and followed, whether or not they're understood. They learn to start from the left when adding, subtracting, and multiplying and to start from the right when dividing. When learning about fractions, they combine the numerators but not the denominators when adding, yet operate on both numerators and denominators when multiplying. Working with decimals, they learn procedures for moving decimal points correctly.

In one way, textbook algorithms are social conventions. They're generalized procedures that people find useful for doing arithmetic. These socially accepted conventions, however, also have underlying logical structures and real purpose. Students often focus on learning to do the procedures in isolation. Missing is attention to understanding the reasons that particular procedures make sense or the contexts of situations for which they're useful. Too often, merely following procedures is what's required and rewarded.

The consequences of this approach have become evident. Students learn and master procedures, yet are not able to apply those procedures to solve problems. This lesson starts with the situations and presents students with the challenge of using percents to make decisions in ways that make sense to them.

I began the lesson by relating an experience I had recently had. I told the students that I had recently gone to a new restaurant for dinner with friends. The service was slow, the waiter was hard to find, and the food was not very good.

"After we had eaten," I said, "my friends and I discussed how much tip to leave. How do your parents tip when they go out for dinner?"

Joey answered quickly. "My dad just leaves the change," he said.

"My dad leaves a buck," Paul contributed, "or sometimes $2.00."

Khalil raised his hand. "My friend's parents leave 10 to 15 percent," he said.

"My parents like to go out to nice restaurants a lot," Jimmy said. "They leave $10.00 to $15.00."

With this introduction, I told them that I had three tipping situations for them to consider in their groups. (See pages 158–159 for these situations.) "Choose one person to read the situation to your group," I said; "then discuss it. Your job is to agree on the percent and the amount of money you would leave for a tip. Also, you need to explain your reasoning in writing. I'll be looking for everyone to be involved in the discussions so that everyone has the opportunity to contribute and learn."

The groups got right to work and the discussions were lively. At one table, Dwight and James were busy arguing while Nam was poking calculator buttons, and Eric was deeply involved in paper-and-pencil calculations. At another table, Alex, Nin, Tony, and Joey had their heads together in earnest discussion.

Gina was the only student in the class who seemed uninvolved. Generally a cooperative student, she seemed listless. I wondered whether she was confused, tired, or simply not interested. I asked her but merely got a shrug. As this was unusual behavior for Gina, I chalked it up to one of the moods that often strike students of this age. I decided not to push, to wait to see if there were changes tomorrow.

After about twenty minutes, most groups seemed to be finished with the three situations. The class discussion revealed that some groups' interaction centered mainly on agreeing on what percent tip to leave. They then figured the amount of money they should leave the waiter or waitress. Figuring didn't pose a problem for the groups as there was always at least one student in each group who was able to do the calculation to the satisfaction of the others. Other groups worked differently, arguing, often quite ferociously, about how much money to leave. They would then figure out what percent of the bill that amount represented.

For the first situation, the fancy dinner with Jason's grandmother, most of the tips groups reported fell in a range of from 15 to 25 percent. Their reasons were all similar to what Martin reported for his group. "We chose a 20 percent tip," he said, "because the service was excellent and the food was terrific."

Peter reported a different decision. When he announced that his group would leave 30 percent, many of the students groaned. At that point, his group mutinied and said that it was Peter's idea so it would be Peter's money. Peter seemed to take pride in being a "big tipper."

Steven then announced that his group would leave 50 percent. The other students in the class were totally disbelieving. Steven defended his position. "$14.90 isn't that much money," he said.

Steven's group was also the most generous for the second situation. They left $10.00, almost a 30 percent tip. They wrote: *Because Sara was a brat, and the waitress didn't get mad at the people, and the food was fine.*

The other groups left either 10 percent or 15 percent. The group with Darren, Sean Paul, Martin, and Dave decided they would leave a 15 percent tip. They wrote: *We left a 15% tip because the food was good, but the service (waitress) wasn't all that good because she didn't have a lot of patience.*

Danelle, Jamie, Alex, and Bryan, however, left a 15 percent tip for a contrasting reason. They wrote: *We decided to give 15 percent because she didn't lose her patience with Sara.*

The third situation was tough for the students because their experiences at pizza parlors most often do not involve waiters or waitresses. Jon, Khalil, and Gina, who hadn't been at all stingy in the previous situations, wrote: *No tip. No kid would give a pizza waitress a tip. Unless their rich.*

Ed, Liz, Paul, and Audrey agreed. They wrote: *Kids usually don't have much money and wouldn't tip much.* The other groups gave the waitress from 15 to 25 percent.

For homework, students were asked to write a restaurant story for others to solve. Their story needed to be one for which two questions could be answered: "What percent tip is reasonable?" "How much money would you leave?" They were to write their answers and explanations for the two questions on a separate sheet of paper. In a later lesson, students exchanged papers, wrote solutions for each other's stories, and then met to compare and discuss their work.

Situation 1

When Jason's grandmother came for a visit, she invited Jason and Diane out for dinner. She told them she'd take them to a special and favorite restaurant of hers and asked that they dress up a bit.

The restaurant was the plushest one that Jason had ever eaten in. The service was amazing to him. First the waiter held the chair for Jason's grandmother to be seated. Then he unfolded her napkin and placed it on her lap. He did the same with Diane and Jason's napkins. Another waiter came over and filled their water glasses. Still another placed a hot roll on each of their bread plates. Jason ate his roll immediately and then ate Diane's, since she was dieting as usual.

The dinner was delicious. Even Diane was impressed, though she ordered only a cup of soup and a small salad. During dinner, Jason had two more rolls. They were hard to resist, especially since the waiter brought a hot one every time Jason's plate was empty. Jason didn't have any room for dessert, but his chicken was terrific. His grandmother said the veal was perfectly prepared.

The bill came to $29.80 without tax. How much tip is reasonable?

Situation 2

Jason's parents decided to take the family out for dinner. Besides themselves, there were Jason, his baby sister, Sara, who was 3 years old, and his older sister, Diane, who was 14. They went to a favorite family restaurant that had something for everyone.

Dinner was fine . . . almost. The only problem was Sara, who hadn't learned about restaurant manners yet. She squirmed in the highchair the

---

waitress brought, spilled her water, threw her fork down twice, and squealed intermittently and loudly.

Jason was a bit embarrassed because he could tell people at other tables were annoyed at the disruption. Jason's mother, however, said that the only way Sara would learn was to have the experience; she avoided the glances of others. Jason's father seemed amused at first, but his smile tightened as the dinner went on. Diane ignored everyone and nibbled on her salad, which was all she was eating for dinner so as not to gain weight.

The waitress was helpful, at least at the onset of the meal. But she seemed to get less sympathetic after cleaning up the spilled water and getting Sara her third fork. Jason's mother thought she was rude; Jason's dad thought she was doing as well as could be expected.

The bill, without tax, came to $33.75. What do you think is a reasonable tip and why?

Situation 3

Jason and three friends went out for pizza after a school basketball game. They ordered two medium pizzas, one pepperoni and one plain. They each ordered a Coke.

The waitress brought their drinks right away, which was great since they were all thirsty from all the cheering they had done at the game. The pizzas were ready very soon, and she brought them right over, with a stack of extra napkins for them to use.

The bill was $13.90 without tax. What is a reasonable tip?

Investigating a Claim From "Harper's Index"

As a regular feature, *Harper's Magazine* includes "Harper's Index," a listing of statistical information about a variety of aspects of the world. An item in the October 1989 (p. 15) issue read:

Percentage of supermarket prices that end in the digit 9 or 5:   80%

I used this statement for a classroom investigation. I had the students collect and analyze data in order to test its validity and then write letters to *Harper's Magazine* describing their results. In this way, the math experience was integrated with a lesson on letter writing.

To prepare for the investigation, I wrote the statement about supermarket prices on an overhead transparency and projected it for the class.

"How might you go about finding out whether or not the statement is true?" I asked.

"You could go to the supermarket and check," Heather said.

"Yeah, but that would only be one market," Jimmy added. "You couldn't check all the markets."

"Still, it would give you a pretty good idea," Heather responded, defending her idea.

"Let's go on a field trip and find out," Jon said. That got a chorus of support from the class.

"Only kidding," Jon added.

"Even if we went to the market," Dwight said, "it would be hard to check every single item. Sometimes they don't even have the prices marked on the shelves. They use those special codes."

"I have an idea," Stephanie said. "You wouldn't have to check every item, but just enough to see how it's going."

"What do you want us to do?" Frank asked. The class looked at me.

"I think collecting data is a first step," I answered. "How about each of you bringing a supermarket receipt to class and then we'll analyze the prices?"

"Is that our homework?" Alex asked.

"Yes," I responded. "Bring in a store receipt by Thursday. That gives you two days in case no one in your family went shopping today. On Thursday, you'll work in your groups to analyze the information on the receipts you've brought."

"Can we bring in more than one?" Melissa asked.

"Yes," I responded. "The more information you have, the more reliable your analysis will be."

All but three students brought receipts to class on Thursday. No group had fewer than three; most had five or six. "Your job as a group," I explained, "is to conduct an investigation to determine whether or not you believe the statement to be true."

I projected guidelines I had written on an overhead transparency.

The product required is a written report of your investigation. It must show:

1. *Results of the data* shown in a neat and organized manner.
2. *Your calculations*, with an explanation about why the particular procedures you use make sense.
3. *Your conclusion*, explained clearly and concisely.

I reviewed the guidelines with the class and then said, "Put your heads together and talk about how you'll analyze what percent of prices end with 9 or 5."

After a few minutes, I interrupted the class and asked groups to share how they were organizing their work. This way, students would hear some options for recording and analyzing their data before committing to a particular way.

Eric reported for his group. "We listed all the numbers prices could end in, from 0 to 9, and now we're making tallies for each price to show what it ended in."

Kim's group was using a different procedure. "I'm reading off the last numbers, and Raymond is writing them down. Then we'll look at our list later."

"We just have two columns," Phi said holding up his group's paper, "one for 9 and 5 and one for other. We're making an X for each price in the right column."

Other groups' methods were the same or a variation of these.

"Before you get back to work," I said, "discuss in your groups whether you want to change your method of organizing or continue as you started. When you've done your analysis, come up and record on the chart I've prepared on the overhead what percent of your prices ended with a 9 or 5. Also, be sure to explain on your paper how you figured the percent."

The students work in groups of four to analyze their supermarket receipts.

The students got back to work. After they all recorded their findings on the transparency, I called the class to attention and asked them to look at our data.

Table Number	Total Number of Items	Number of Items Ending with 5 or 9	Percent of Items Ending with 5 or 9
6	118	59	50.0
2	190	120	63.0
4	100	70	70.0
1	43	26	60.5
3	202	126	63.0
5	144	66	54.2
7	97	39	32.0

"Well, what do you think?" I asked. I gave all the students who volunteered a chance to express their ideas.

"I think we should find out if they used different supermarkets," Dwight said.

"Maybe where the magazine is published, the prices are different," Kim said.

"Half of the groups figured that between 60 and 70 percent of the prices ended with 9 or 5," Teddy reported.

"But all the groups' results were lower than 80 percent," Melissa added.

"What do you think might account for the difference between our statistics and the claim from Harper's?" I asked.

"I know," Jimmy blurted out. He had been studying his groups' receipts. "All the ones that didn't end in 9 or 5 are meats or fruits or vegetables. Maybe they didn't count them." The others examined their receipts and came to the same conclusion.

"No fair," Dwight said. "They should have said if they weren't counting meat or vegetables."

The period was almost over. Sometimes the time allotted to class periods passes all too quickly. There was no time to continue with the investigation or discuss the methods the groups used for their calculations.

"We'll continue tomorrow," I said. "Please hand in your groups' papers and receipts before your leave."

I looked at the groups' papers that night to see how they had arrived at the percents they reported. Since I hadn't taught them an algorithm for figuring out what percent one number is of another, I was curious about the reasoning processes they used.

Table 3 figured that 126 was 63 percent of 202. They wrote: *We found that there were about 200 items and 126 had a 9 or a 5. Our group figured that for 200 it takes 2 to equil 1%. Then we drew 126 lines because that was how many were 9 or 5 and circled every 2 lines and it came out to 63%.*

Table 2 collected data in two columns. For each receipt, they put the total number of items in one column and the number of items that ended with 5 or 9 in the other. They added and found they had 190 items in all, of which 120 ended in 5 or 9. They then constructed a chart:

$$100\% = 190$$
$$50\% = 95$$
$$25\% = 47.5$$
$$20\% = 38$$
$$10\% = 19$$
$$5\% = 9.50$$
$$1\% = 1.9$$

By adding different combinations of percents together, using a trial and error approach, they figured that 63 percent represented 119.7 items. They concluded: *We got 63% because after adding the percents the number came close to 120.*

Table 4 listed the digits from 1 to 9 and made a tally for each item to show how many ended in each digit. Their problem was simple because they had exactly 100 items on their receipts. They wrote: *Each tally is worth one percent. So there is 100 percent. There are 70 total numbers with nine and fives. So there are 70% of the total numbers are fives and nine.*

Table 6 also had friendly numbers with which to work. Their four receipts produced 59 items that ended with 5 or 9 and 118 items in all. They reported 50 percent because 59 is half of 118.

Table 1 had 43 items with 26 ending in 9 or 5. They wrote: *First we went 43 into a hundred on a calculator to find out how much each price was worth. Each price was worth 2.3255813%. So we went 26 times 2.3255813 on a calculator. So the answer is 60.5% end in 5 or 9. Our group thinks that harpers magazine answer was too high, but they are probably right because we only did this report on 4 receipts.*

Table 5 used faulty reasoning and arrived at an incorrect answer. Of their 144 items, 66 ended with 9 or 5. They wrote: *We took 66 over 144 and we took 66 multiplied by 100 which equals 6,600 divided by 144 which equals 45.83. Then we took 100* minus 45.83 and we got 54.16 and we rounded it off. That's how we got the answer which is 54.2.

Table 7 used a very complicated procedure that involved rounding, dividing, subtracting, multiplying, and adding in ways that made no sense to me. The group came to the incorrect conclusion that 39 of 97 items represented 32 percent.

I decided that in the next class, I would have the groups continue their investigation, this time dealing with the meat, fruits, and vegetables differently. While they were working, I would talk with tables 5 and 7 about their reasoning.

I began class the next day by having Kim, Jimmy, and Dwight repeat the ideas they had offered about why the class results differed from the Harper's statement. I then showed the class an item I had copied on a transparency from one of the receipts.

Celery   .92
1.87 LB @ .49/LB

Step I:

11	20. 5 or 9's
27	13 5 or 9's
30	27 5 or 9's
62	60 5 or 9's

Step II:

Total = 190   Total 9's and 5's = 120

(percentage)

100% = 190	60% —▶ 114
50% = 95	70% —▶ 133
25% = 47.5	65% —▶ 123.5
20% = 38	64% —▶ 121.6
10% = 19	63% —▶ 119.7
5% = 9.50	
1% = 1.9	

Step III: Operation makes sense because you can add the percents together and then with the numbers it equals too.

(conclusion)
Step IV: We got 63% because after adding the percents the number came close to 120.

Table 2 used trial and error and added different combinations of percents together to arrive at their answer of 63%.

Our group disagrees with the little answer. We think it is much lower than 80%. Our group thinks it is 63% of the bill would be the answer.
We got 63% by adding up all of the items on the bill then we found all of the items that ended in a 9 or a 5. Then we found that there were about 200 items and 126 hadle a 9 or a 5. Our group figured that for 200 it takes 2 to equil 1%. Then we drew 126 lines because that was howmany were 9 or 5 and circled every 2 lines and it came out to 63%.

Ted, Ron, and Cathy explained why they disagree with the "Harper's Index" claim.

"Who can interpret this for the class?" I asked. Audrey explained that 1.87 pounds of celery at $.49 per pound cost $.92.

"I noticed from looking at the receipts," I said, "that the price per pound of meat, fruits, and vegetables usually ended with a 9 or 5, but the total price paid usually didn't. Maybe the researcher for the "Harper's Index" considered the price per pound rather than the price paid."

"We need to do it again," Kim said. Others also expressed interest.

I then asked, "In your first analysis, you included the $.92 in your data. This time, which will you do, include the price of $.49 per pound or eliminate the celery? Discuss this in your groups."

All but one group felt that $.49 should be included. Craig reported for his group. "The statement is about supermarket prices, and celery is a price," he said, "so we shouldn't eliminate it."

Stephanie said, "We think we should stick with everything on the receipt. It doesn't seem right to cross some off."

Eddie said, "We should go with the price per pound because that's the only way we'll know if it's 80 percent of all prices."

Teddy reported his group's view. "We don't think we should count the meat or fruit or vegetables at all," he said. They had no specific reason to account for their idea that this was the best choice.

Because I had stuffed all their receipts in an envelope, there was no way to be sure each group got their own receipts again. This sparked a discussion about whether the results would be valid if they didn't have the same receipts.

"We have to have the same number of items to be accurate," Dwight said.

"We want to be able to compare with what we had before," Kim said.

"My name is on mine," Melissa said, "and I think most people would like their same ones back."

"It seems you'd like to use your own receipts," I said, "but since that isn't possible I'm going to distribute the receipts at random. We'll compile class results at the end."

"What about Teddy's group?" Jon asked. "Are you going to let them not count the meat and fruit and vegetables?"

Heather, a member of Teddy's group, responded. "We'll be able to see if it matters," she said.

I posted the guidelines I had written for the first investigation and reviewed them with the class. I then distributed the receipts.

As the groups got organized, I talked with table 5 about their work. "One step of what you did yesterday didn't make sense to me," I began. "Help me understand your reasoning. There were 66 of your 144 items that ended in 5 or 9. Right?"

"Right," Jimmy answered. The others nodded.

"So it seems you figured that 66 of 144 was 45.83 percent," I continued.

"Yeah," Mervin explained. "We did 66 times 100 because percent is 100 and then divided by 144."

"Why did you subtract your answer from 100 to get 54.2?" I asked. They were stumped.

Kim then said, "That doesn't make sense. It tells how much percent the others were. See, we didn't need to do that." The others seemed confused.

"I agree with Kim," I said, "but it's important for each of you to understand this. Talk about it before you start the new investigation."

When I left them, there were questions from several other tables. Some receipts didn't indicate the price per pound for meat, and the students wanted to know what to do. I told them they should do what they thought was best and be sure to mention this in their report.

Then I went to talk with table 7. Rather than have them try and reconstruct the logic of their complicated procedure, I decided to focus on the sense of their answer.

"I'm perplexed by what you did to arrive at 32 percent," I began. They giggled.

"See if you can understand my thinking," I continued. "You had 97 items with 39 ending in 5 or 9. Suppose we rounded each of those numbers to friendlier numbers to do some mental figuring. What numbers could I use?"

Norberto answered, "You change 97 to 100 and 39 to 40."

"OK," I said. "Then about $^{40}/_{100}$ of the items end in 9 or 5. What percent is 40 of 100?"

"That's easy," Elena said, "it's 40 percent."

"I agree," I said. "That's why I don't think your answer of 32 percent makes sense."

"Well, it's close," Paul said.

"Yes," I responded, "but I don't think it's close enough. Besides, I think you made some errors in your thinking. Look at your first paragraph. One receipt had 13 out of 19 items that ended with a 5 or 9. You said that if you rounded 19 to 20, you'd need to multiply by 5 to change the 20 to 100. If you make the 19 about 5 times larger, you need to do the same with 13, and 13 times 5 is 65. So $^{13}/_{19}$ is about the same as $^{65}/_{100}$, which is 65 percent, not 89 percent, as you figured." I wrote this down for them.

"I think you need to rethink your procedures for this next investigation," I said. Though I didn't think they understood, I left them to discuss it among themselves.

It was now near the end of the period, and all the groups indicated that they needed more time to finish. "You can use the beginning of tomorrow's class," I

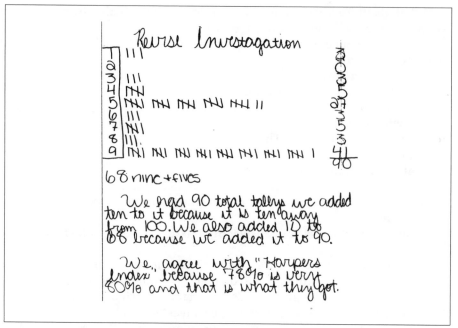

Having students write helps identify misconceptions. In this paper, the students show confusion about reasoning proportionally.

told them. I collected their work, this time having them use paper clips to attach the receipts they were using to their papers.

It was hard to settle the class the next day. The school schedule is a rotating one, and this was the last period in the day. It's often a real challenge to motivate students at this time. The classroom reeked of Corn Nuts. Sheila was busily putting on makeup. Elena was teasing her hair. Teddy was sitting on top of a desk. Eddie and Mervin were teasing each other. The class was noisy and unfocused. It was difficult to get their attention.

Finally they were ready for me to begin. I returned their papers and receipts and said, "Check and double-check your work, write your reports, and enter your data on the overhead transparency. You have fifteen minutes to accomplish this." My directive moved them to action.

"When your group finishes," I said, "check the other groups' percents to make sure you agree."

As the groups were preparing their final reports, I noticed that there was generally one recorder in each group madly writing while the others were relaxing, chatting, or fooling around. I interrupted the class and pointed out what I saw. I asked for suggestions.

Kim said, "I think the whole group should discuss what the person should write and then one person should tell the writer what to put down."

Jimmy said, "Yeah, and the other two people could check it over after."

Others in the class nodded. There were no other suggestions. The class was much more organized after this conversation.

When table 1 posted their data, they began to question their entry of 57.0 percent (28 of 49 items) when they noticed that what had already been recorded were 72.0 percent, 67.5 percent, and 78.0 percent. They had explained their reasoning clearly. They wrote: *There were 49 items and 28 9 or 5's. We took 100 be-*

cause it was a whole. We divided it by 49 to find out how many 49's were in 100. It came out to: 2.0408163. Then we multiplied it by 28 because there are 28 items that end with 9 or 5's. We multiplied to find the percent of the recipts. We got 57%.

"Look," Jon said, "the other percents are much higher."

"Yeah, but look how many more items they had," Steven said. The first three entries had samples of 165, 80, and 90 items.

Jon stared at the screen. Finally, he said, "It's probably the more on the receipts, the bigger the percents are."

"Yeah, probably," Alex agreed.

Overhearing their conversation made me aware of how fragile students' understanding of concepts can be. They need many, many experiences from which to construct, elaborate, and deepen their learning.

I looked at some of the groups' reports. For the first investigation, table 4 had correctly reported that 70 was 70 percent of 100. However, they revealed their confusion with the new data. Now they had 90 items with 68 ending in 9 or 5. What they did was add 10 to the 90 to get 100, and then add 10 to 68 to get 78. They knew about relating percent to 100 but not about doing so proportionally. This reminded me to beware being seduced by right answers into making false assumptions about what students understand. Also, I was reminded that partial understanding and periods of confusion are part of the learning process.

Table 5 figured their percent correctly this time and were able to explain their reasoning clearly. Table 7, however, was still confused.

I focused the class on the results of their second investigations.

Table Number	Total Number of Items	Number of Items Ending with 5 or 9	Percent of Items Ending with 5 or 9
3	165	120	72.00
6	80	54	67.50
4	90	68	78.00
1	49	28	57.00
2	190	134	70.00
5	85	50	59.00
7	133	75	53.25

I hadn't had students share their methods for finding percents with each other. I know that following other people's reasoning is difficult, and I didn't feel listening to others' methods would benefit the students. Instead, I decided to have all the groups analyze the same data and use the totals for the entire class.

I asked the students to figure out the total number of items on everyone's receipts and the total number of items that ended with 9 or 5. There were 792 items in all and 529 that ended with 9 or 5.

"Discuss in your groups how you would figure out what percent 529 is of 792," I said. "Then you'll report your ideas so we can see the different ways of figuring."

"Do we have to write it down?" Alex asked.

"Only if it helps you figure," I said.

Their discussions were animated. Teddy reported for his group. "You have to go down from 792 to 100, which you do by dividing by 7.92," he said. "So then we divided 529 by 7.92 and got 66.7 percent."

"We got an answer that's close but not exact," Stephanie reported. "We said that 792 was about 800, and that's 8 times more than 100. So we divided 529 by 8 and got 66.1 percent."

"It's hard when the numbers are so big," Elena reported for her group.

"Does it make sense for the answer to be more than 50.0 percent?" I asked. "Talk about that in your group."

For most of the students that made sense. "Because 500 is more than half of 800," Jimmy explained.

"How would you do it?" Norberto asked me.

"I'd use a calculator," I answered. "Let me see if this makes sense. If there were 2 items and 1 ended in a 9 or 5, what percent would that be?"

Several students answered 50.0 percent. Others nodded.

"Yes," I said, "1 out of 2 is 50.0 percent. I can do that on the calculator by doing 1 divided by 2 and pressing the percent key. Try it. You'll get 50." I gave them a moment to verify this procedure.

"But why do you divide?" Melissa asked.

I answered by referring to money. "Half a dollar," I said, "is the same as dividing $1.00 in 2. ½ means the same as 1 divided by 2."

"So what do you divide for the problem?" Dwight asked.

"I know the fraction of items that end in 9 or 5," I said, and wrote $^{529}\!/_{792}$ on the board. "So I divide 529 by 792 and press the percent key."

There were a variety of reactions as the students tried this. "Neat!" "That's easy." "I don't get it." "Does it always work?" "That's much easier." "It should be 66.8, not 66.7."

"So we proved Harper's wrong," Darren said.

"Your homework assignment is to write to the editor of *Harper's Magazine*," I said. I had prepared guidelines for them to follow that I distributed for each student. The guidelines stated that they were to support their opinions with evidence. Also, they could include problems that came up during their research that might have caused a discrepancy, and they could offer suggestions for rephrasing the statement. They had three days for this assignment.

I also talked to them about the proper form for a business letter. I gave them each a sample letter as a model and talked with them about the heading, inside address, greeting, body, closing, and signature.

"Will we mail these letters?" Martin wanted to know.

"I'll check them first. Then I'll mail a packet of the letters any of you want to send."

When I read their letters, I used Post-its to make comments and give initial grades. I decided to have a class discussion to help the students understand what I thought was high-quality work. Then I would give the students a chance to revise their letters.

I wrote the following outline on an overhead:

Introduction
Description of our investigation
Explanation of the problem we
    encountered + how we changed
    our procedure
Support of statements with data
Closing

> ### What I learned About Doing the "Harper's" Investagation
>
> I learned that if someone in a big business like that or a newspaper makes a percentage based on a survey like that you shouldn't just believe it check it and make sure. And for some reason the percentages are easier to understand to me, and I hope it has prepared me for later in life experiences. Thank you

Melissa wrote about what she learned from the "Harper's Index" investigation.

For each area on my outline, I made a list of which students' letters provided exemplary samples. I began class by talking with the students about the importance of organizing their thoughts and expressing them clearly. Then I returned their letters to them and gave them a chance to read my comments.

"When I read your letters," I said, "I made a list of which ones were high-quality examples for each category on the outline. I'd like you to hear what others wrote. Then you'll have the chance to rewrite your letters if you wish."

I showed them the outline I had written and asked some students to read parts of their letters. For example, I had students read the following examples of closing paragraphs.

Nathan wrote: *We think our results are different from yours for several reasons. With items purchased by the pound, we weren't sure if we should use the price per pound or the total price. We also had a very small sample of receipts, only 30. We are not sure we would get the same results with a larger sample. We also are not sure what kinds of stores you used. That might make a difference too.*

Stephanie wrote: *We realize that there are less of our receipts than you looked at and we live in a different part of the United States than you so that might make a difference. It just made us curious. Thank you.*

From Melissa: *Your article provided us with a very interesting class project. We know our sampling size was small and limited to the local supermarkets and that is probably why our percentages differ. This has also raised a question in my mind of why these prices end with 9's or 5's and we are still discussing it in my class.*

This went well. Students were interested in hearing how others expressed themselves. "Your final letters are due tomorrow," I then said. "I'll reread them, reevaluate them if you've made revisions, and give final grades. If you make revisions, please hand in both versions. Also, indicate if you'd like your letter sent."

About a third of the class did some revisions on their letters. Jimmy's "P.S." at the end of his letters summed up my broad goal for this activity: *I learned from this investigation that I can find and investigate something interesting and see if its right or wrong and explain why it is right or wrong.*

Assessing Students' Understanding (So Far)

Assessing what students know is essential for making instructional decisions. It's important to have a sense of what students understand on an ongoing basis so that the students' needs define the curriculum, rather than a prescribed set of activities or textbook pages.

I learn about what my students understand in three ways. I observe their group interactions during lessons. I listen to what they say in class discussions. I read their written assignments from class work and homework. At times I ask students to write specifically about what they understand, sometimes for homework and sometimes as a class assignment. Writing gives students the chance to reflect on their own learning and provides information to me about their thinking. This homework assignment is an example of such an assessment.

"I'm interested in finding out what you now know about percents," I told the students. "What I'd like you to do for homework is to write a paper titled 'What I Know About Percent (So Far).'" I wrote this title on an overhead transparency.

"Why do you think I added 'So Far' to the title?" I asked.

"Because we're not finished learning yet," Darshana said.

"Because you want to know where we are now," Frank added.

"Because it's not like a final test," Kim said.

"Yes, those are some of my reasons," I said. "Also, in order to plan more activities for you, I'd like to have as good a sense as possible of what each of you knows."

"How much do we have to write?" Raymond asked.

"What I'm interested in," I responded, "is getting as complete a picture as possible of what you understand. I imagine that will take a full page, more or less. What's important is that you include as many details as possible."

"Should we tell how we solve problems?" Nam asked.

"If that will give me information about your thinking and understanding, then it would be helpful," I answered. "The more information you provide, the better."

In their papers, students included information about what percents are, situations in which percents are used, and ways to represent them. Darshana, for example, wrote: *I know that percent is used for many things. It is used for grading, weather, tiping, and survaying. I learned how to estamate more accurly. I also learned that 100 is the main factor in percents. That means a pie is 100% or 2% means .02 hundredths. Fractions are related to percents. That means ½ is also 50%. Some good ways to figure out percents are pencil and paper, calculator, and your mind.*

Dwight wrote: *I know that percent has to do with decimals. You can make a decimal into a percentage. Percent is used in odds, for example 60% rain and 20% humidity. Percents are used every day in the United States. When sports announcers announce sports they see what team has a better percentage of winning the game. Percentage also has to do with 100. I think the term "percent" is an easier way of figuring out a problem.*

Some students also included ways of calculating. For example, Eric wrote: *I know that percent is a type of ratio. Percent is used to figure out how many out of one hundred something is. Like what percent of a hundred apples are green or yellow or red. People use percent in all sorts of ways. Such as figuring out budgets for vacations, the chance of rain, and how much of what is in the air. Percentage is used for many other*

What I Know About Percent (So far)

I know that percent has to do with decimals. You can make a decimal into a percentage. Percent is used in odds, for example 60% rain and 20% humidity. Percents are used every day in the United States. When sports announcers announce sports they see what team has a better percentage of winning the game. Percentage also has to do with 100. I think the term "percent" is an easier way of figuring out a problem.

What I Know About Percent
(So Far)

I know that percent is a type of ratio. Percent is used to figure out how many out of one-hundred something is. Like what percent of a hundred apples are green or yellow or red.

People use percent in all sorts of ways. Such as figuring out budgets for vacations, the chance of rain, and how much of what is in the air.

Percentage is used for many other things in our world too. Percent is a simple, accurate way to figure things out

Here is a table to help with percent

50% of 500 is 250
25% of 500 is 125
10% of 500 is 50
5% of 500 is 25
1% of 500 is 5

Students' writing is useful for assessing their understanding.

> What I know about percent (so far)
>
> I know that if there were 100 ~~things~~ dollars each would count for 1%. Percent can go up too 100%, and sometimes over. If there were less or more than 100 dollars, and you wanted to figure out the percent, you would figure out first, what each dollar would equal in per cent. Sometimes when your figuring what each dollar counts for in %, it doesn't come out even. When this happenes, you just estimate, or round-off. Percent doesn't always have to be related to money. you can figure out percents of anything. A percent is the fraction of a whole number.

things in our world too. *Percent is a simple, accurate way to figure things out. Here is a table to help with percent.*

50% of 500 is 250

25% of 500 is 125

10% of 500 is 50

5% of 500 is 25

1% of 500 is 5

Lemuel wrote: *What I know is that it has to do with 100 and if you want to find out a percent of something like what is 1% of $500 you could use a calculator to multiply $500 by .01 which equals to $5.00 or if it's easy enough to do in your head you don't need to use a calculator. You can also use percent to find out how many students in this school are right handers and how many are left handers, etc.*

Heather wrote: *What I know about percent so far is that you use it when you are tipping a waitress, figuring out a sale and weather forecasting. I know that 50% of something is half and 25% of something is one fourth. Percents can be changed from fractions. Also if 60% of rain is predicted one day and 40% the next I know that doesn't mean a 100% chance of rain. And if you get a 90% on a test it means you're doing real well and got an A−. I also know that in order to find 20% of a $34.00 tip you must divide $34.00 by five because 5 times 20% equals 100%. So 20% of $34.00 is $6.80.*

One issue that appeared in several students' papers was how large percents can be. Nam, for example, began his paper with: *I know that the maximum percent is 100.* Jena, however, began her paper with: *I know that if there were 100 dollars each would count for 1%. Percent can go up to 100%, and sometimes over.* Nin wrote: *Parts of a whole have to sum up to 100%. The percent of a whole is 100%. Doubling will* be 100% more. Tripling will be 200% more and so on. Tony wrote: *I know that percent is what a number is out of 100. There is no percent higher than 100%.*

Some students wrote about difficulties they were having. Tony also included in his paper: *I know that $25 is twenty-five percent out of $100. I know that ⅕ is 20% out of 100%. I also know that percents are used everywhere and alot of the time. Some problems that I have with percents are the ones I don't understand. For example 13% out of $15.00. Or 23 percent out of $300.00. These problems and some problems like these are the ones I don't really understand. I guess the ones I don't understand are the ones that have an odd number for a percent.*

Jon wrote: *The first thing I think about when I hear percent is 100%. I know that most of the time when you want to find how percent of something is you usually use 100%. I also know that there are many ways to get answers and that is when I get confused. Sometimes I know how to do it and sometimes I don't. Percent to me is a guess or an estimate and later you try to find the real percent. I think percent is kind of easy and hard.*

Stephanie wrote: *So far all I know about percent is that it is very confusing! I think I understand how to solve a percent problem but since we didn't do percents last year this is my first time doing percents I am easily confused when a new way to solve a problem pops out at me. Here is an example of what I think when you ask what 20% means to me. Well if you take a dollar you know that there are 100 pennies in that dollar. And when you have that 100% that means that each penny stands for 1% so 20% of a dollar is 20 cents.*

From reading the students' papers, I learned about the range of students' understandings. I learned from the references to the possible maximum size of percents that this issue needed attention in class. I learned from the many references to money that it seemed to help students think about percents.

The challenge of teaching is what to do with this information. I've come to know that partial understanding and confusion are natural to the process of learning. I believe that students need to figure out ways to make an idea such as percents make sense to them and that teaching by telling doesn't always support this.

My decision was to continue with more problem-solving experiences. I included more discussions from class graphs, in which we focused on analyzing data using percents. I used questions for the graphs that drew from the students' daily experiences: "How many hours a day do you watch TV? If you could only watch TV one night of the week, which night would you choose?" "Which is your favorite fast-food restaurant?" "Is your hair straight, wavy, or curly?" "Do you have moons on any of your fingernails?" "How many glasses of milk do you drink each day?"

I continued to have students share their methods for finding percents. I showed them methods I use, doing so with a light touch and encouraging them to use only those methods that made sense to them. I kept surrounding them with percents in many different ways. Following are a few more of the class activities I did.

A Situation from Real Life—The Hamburger Problem

A newspaper advertisement presented another contextual situation for the students' study of percents. A local hamburger place included a coupon in their advertisement that gave $ .70 off the regular price of a hamburger, fries, and a large Coke. The regular price was $3.59. I thought that the students could investigate what percent discount the coupon gave.

This one coupon is good for everyone in your group.

Actually, this is a standard type of word problem but one that has the hook of relating to the students' own experiences. The lesson models how such a standard type of problem can be used for learning through application rather than applying after learning.

To prepare for the lesson, I made an overhead transparency of the coupon and wrote underneath:

About what percent discount do you get with this coupon?

I asked the students to work on this problem with their group. Then I had someone from each group present his or her group's method. On an overhead transparency, I recorded the methods they used.

Alex reported for his group. "We divided 3.59 by 100 to find out how much 1 percent was and got .035," he said. "Then we messed around to find out how many .035s it took to make $2.89. We figured about 80. That means $2.89 was 80 percent of the cost so the discount was 20%." Alex didn't explain that the $2.89 came from subtracting $.70 from $3.59, but it wasn't necessary as everyone had figured that out.

Marshay explained what her group did. "We used the calculator," she said. "We did 3.59 minus 30 percent and got 2.51, and that was too much. So we did 3.59 minus 25 percent, and it was still too much. We did 3.59 minus 20 percent, and it was really close."

Steven said, "We did $.70 divided by $3.59 and got .194986 so we rounded it to 20 percent. We used a calculator."

Craig reported, "We subtracted $3.59 minus $.70 and got $2.89 and then divided $2.89 by $3.59 and got about 80, which is 80 percent, so 100 percent minus 80 percent equals 20 percent discount."

Nin reported for his group. He said, ".70 divided by 3.59 is .19 and something which is close to .20, so that equals ⅕, so the discount is 20 percent."

Tamika described what her group did. "We made a chart," she said. "We figured 100 percent of 3.59, 50 percent of 3.59, and then 25 percent, 10 percent, and 1 percent. Then we added different amounts. We added 25 percent plus 50 percent plus 5 percent and got about 2.89. That was 80 percent altogether, so the discount was 20 percent."

Dwight was the last to report. "We did it kind of like Tamika did," he said. "We made the chart and knew that 25 percent was about $.89 and 5 percent was about $.18, so 25 percent minus 5 percent was about $.70. So we knew it was a 20 percent discount."

I then gave the groups a few minutes to record another way to figure the discount that made sense to them and that was different from the way they had solved it.

The problem I gave them was a fairly standard type of word problem. However, rather than using it as an assignment, I used it to initiate a discussion that could add to students' repertoire of methods for approaching a problem with percents. In this way, the word problem was used as an opportunity for learning, not as a test.

Geometry, Measurement, and Percents—The Xerox Problem

This problem was inspired by my experience with copying machines. I often reduce or enlarge things for overhead transparencies or to fit conveniently into envelopes. Typically, I take a chance on the percent of reduction or enlargement. Typically, I'm wrong and have to try again. It occurred to me that doing some figuring with percents would be both a more elegant way to solve such problems and certainly less wasteful of paper. A classroom application for this situation then occurred to me. This problem relates geometry and measurement to the study of percents, still in a contextual setting.

I prepared a packet of six sheets for each group of four students. I copied a cartoon I had clipped several years ago and drew a 5-by-5-inch square around it. I then made four reductions and one enlargement of it, putting each different size on a different-colored paper. I duplicated a copy of the original and of each of the copies for each group.

I showed the class what I had done. "Your problem," I said, "is to figure out what percent reduction or enlargement I used for each."

I gave each group a packet containing the 100 percent copy and four of the five copies. I kept one of the reductions to offer groups when they were ready for more. "Record your solution for each color and explain how you arrived at it," I said.

"Are we allowed to use rulers to measure?" Jimmy asked. I answered yes. There were no other questions. I gave each group a packet and the students got to work.

Groups' methods differed. One of the reductions was a 3.5-by-3.5-inch square. One group found the answer by doing the following calculations.

$$3.5 \times 5 \ = 17.50$$
$$3.5 \div 5 \ = \ .70$$
$$5 \ \div 3.5 = \ 1.42$$

They wrote: *Since the copy is smaller the only answer that makes sense is 70%*. They used this method for each of the other sizes, each time explaining their rationale for choosing the sensible answer.

Another group arrived at the same answer in a different way. They wrote: *White was 5 inches long and that is 100%. 5 ÷ 100 = 20%. So one inch equals 20%.* They then multiplied 3.5 by 20 to get 70 percent. This method was used by two other groups in the class as well.

A third group wrote: *Measure by inches, then times by 2, then add a 0 after.* They did not explain, however, why that method made sense. When I asked them, Dwight revealed what they had done.

"We didn't know how to do it," he said. "So we looked at the answers Nin's group got, and then we figured a way to get those answers."

"How did you figure out that way?" I asked. They shrugged.

"I think Dwight figured it out," Tamika said. I turned to Dwight.

"I don't know," he said. "I think I just noticed it."

"Do you think it would work for all enlargements and reductions?" I asked further.

Dwight wasn't sure. The others weren't either.

I then distributed the other reduction for them to try. "Figure this one in at least two different ways," I told them. This gave groups a chance to apply others' methods and gave Dwight's group a chance to test their method again.

Having Students Write Story Problems

Textbooks provide story problems for students to solve. I prefer, however, to have students write their own problems. I'm interested in learning what sorts of situations they think of when writing about percents. Also, the problems they write tell me what sorts of problems they feel comfortable solving. Students then solve their own problems.

I asked the class to write a story problem for homework. "Your story problem must meet two criteria," I said. "It must end with a question, and the question must require using percents to answer it. You also have to solve your problems. Do that on a a separate page, showing your work and including an explanation of why your method makes sense."

I began class the next day by having students exchange papers and solve others' problems. "Compare both your solutions and the methods you used," I said. "Let me know if you aren't able to agree on a solution or if you don't understand someone else's method."

I find that solving others' problems motivates students more than solving textbook problems. I think this is because they're interested in what others have written. Also, the chance to talk with each other about methods of solution serves to strengthen and expand what they understand.

The students' problems presented a variety of situations and also varied in complexity. Following are some examples.

Kim wrote: *In a class of twenty-nine students, ten get an allowance of $15.00 weekly, twelve more get an allowance of $10.00 weekly. Five more get an allowance of $5.00 weekly, and only two get no allowance at all. Which percentage of the class do you think gets paid under $500.00 yearly?*

Frank wrote: *Piedmont Middle School scored one hundred points in the whole game. I scored twenty-six out of the thirty-eight I attempted. What is the percent of my shooting 38 and making 26?*

Liz wrote: *When Crystal went to Nordstroms she saw a cute, blue summer dress. She wants to buy the dress but she has to buy lunch too. The dress cost $34.00 and it was marked down 20%. If she only has $29.00 will she have enough money for lunch and the summer dress. If yes, how much would Crystal have left for lunch?*

James wrote: *My dad was in a real good mood last night. He took us to a Chinese restaurant. As we got there, the place was beautiful. The service was wonderful. The food was great. Everything was so good that I began to hog my food. The bill was $53.00. I was thinking of leaving a 25% tip. My dad brought with us $75.00. Will he be able to pay?*

Eddie wrote: *In a day there are 24 hours. Some people sleep about 8 hours in a day. I would like to know about what percent they sleep in a day.*

Comparing Advertisements

The students' story problems about shopping gave me an idea for another classroom activity. The Sunday newspaper comes with several supplements that advertise sales. Some advertisements indicate the percent the consumer will save and others give the sale price. I was interested in seeing how students would compare information to decide on good buys.

I clipped three advertisements. One showed a pair of earrings, listing the sale price of $36.40 and the regular price of $52.00. Another was for a diet scale that cost $7.00 on sale and $10.00 regularly. Neither of these gave the percent of discount. The third offered a 20 percent savings on a toaster oven that was regularly $65.00. I cut the ad so the actual price wasn't included.

I pasted the advertisements on a sheet of paper and duplicated a copy for each group. "Your job is to decide which of these three gives the consumer the best deal," I said. "What information from these ads will be useful for making this decision? Discuss this among yourselves for a minute, and then I'll ask for your ideas."

A small group discussion helps to focus students on the problem.

I find it helpful to have students talk in small groups and then report to the class before they get to work on a problem. The small group discussion focuses them on the problem; the class discussion provides the additional benefit of other ideas and viewpoints.

I called the class back to attention. "What information will you consider in deciding which is the best buy?" I asked.

"We think you should figure out how much you save on each," Eric reported for his group.

"You have to figure out how much percent off each one is," Tony added.

"We think it depends on what you want to buy," Kim said, "I mean, like a girl would buy the earrings, but someone on a diet might want the scale." There was a ripple of laughter in response to Kim's statement.

"It also matters how much money you have to spend," Joey said.

"What about tax?" Melissa said. "You have to pay tax."

"Any other ideas?" I asked. There were none, so I gave the class directions. "Decide as a group which is the best deal. Explain your decision in writing and prepare to present it to the class."

The students' initial ideas pointed out that there's more to making a decision about a purchase than merely comparing prices. This sort of problem is valuable for students as it presents them with a situation that reflects the typical ambiguity of real life situations. I was interested in hearing the groups' decisions. After about fifteen minutes, I began a class discussion.

"We think the earrings are the best to buy," Stephanie said. "It's about the same percent discount as the scale, but it's more savings. It's $15.60 instead of $3.00."

"We sort of agree," Percy reported. "If you do it by percents, the earrings and the diet scale are the best deals. But if you do it by price, the earrings are best because you save the most."

"How did you figure that the earrings offered a 30 percent discount?" I asked.

Eric reported. "I doubled $52.00 and got around $100.00," he said. "So I doubled $36.40. Well, I kind of estimated it and got $70.00. So if $70.00 is 70 percent of $100, the discount is 30 percent."

"See, I told you," Liz hissed at Tony. "You have to minus to get the discount." Tony had argued in his group that the earrings gave a 70 percent discount. He looked a little embarrassed.

"OK, I get it," he mumbled. Liz started making changes on her group's report.

"We did it differently," Audrey said. She came up to the overhead projector and showed what she had written:

$$50\% = \$26$$
$$25\% = \$13$$
$$10\% = \$5.20$$
$$5\% = \$2.60$$

"We figured out that you save $15.60 on the earrings," she continued. "Then I figured different percents and you get $15.60 by adding 25 percent and 5 percent."

"We just did it by guessing and checking on the calculator," Joey said, reporting for a third group. "We figured you save $15.60. We multiplied 25 percent and $52.00 and got $13.00, and that wasn't enough. We tried 30 percent, and we were right. We think the toaster oven is the worst deal because it's only 20 percent off, but the others are 30 percent off."

Kim then explained her group's decision. It was an extension of the thought she presented during the class discussion. Kim is a confident student who effectively lobbies in a group for her ideas. "The earrings are definitely best," she said. "We know you get the same discount on the scale, but it's a dumb thing to buy. Just eat less if you need to lose weight. Besides, the earrings look like better quality."

"Does any group have a different idea?" I asked. ·

Heather raised her hand. She reported what her group had written. "We think the toaster is the best deal because you can use it, and you can clean it really easy," she read. "Also, you can cook anything in there. It is $13.00 off for the sale price. It really looks nice and always will. It can also bake, broil, and toast." She was grinning, obviously pleased with the report. There were laughter and some comments from the class.

I gave the class a few minutes at the end of the period to make changes on their reports. I tell the students often that the rule in class is that you can change your mind whenever you like as long as you can explain your reasoning. This rule encourages students to reflect on their thinking and make sense of things rather than merely to arrive at answers.

A Group Quiz—The Warehouse Problem

This problem appears in the book, *Thinking Mathematically* by John Mason, Leone Burton, and Kaye Stacey (1982). The book offers a rich collection of problems and is also a useful resource for learning to approach solving mathematics problems. This particular problem presents a situation that is counterintuitive for some people. What people initially think makes sense isn't so, and percents are needed to reason this through.

I wrote the following on a worksheet: "For the following problem, explain your thinking clearly on the lines below. Show all work that helps to make your explanation clear."

Underneath these directions, I wrote the warehouse problem: "In a warehouse, you get a 20 percent discount, but you must pay 15 percent sales tax. Which would you prefer to have calculated first, the discount or the tax?"

I gave this to the students as a group quiz. I think there's a minimal distinction between a small group assessment, such as this quiz, and a class activity, such as the hamburger or school bus problems. The distinction lies in my purpose. Giving this problem as a group quiz meant that there was no class discussion and that the students' solutions had to be complete enough so I could assess what they understood. I often find that a group quiz is a good way to prepare students for an individual quiz to follow.

Grading quizzes such as this is more complex than merely checking whether answers are right or wrong. It's clear when a paper earns an A. The conclusion is correct, and the explanation provides substantial evidence. Awnica, Percy, and Melissa calculated the results for a $100.00 item. Then they wrote: *We preferred to do the discount first then the sales tax because it seems you would be going backwards. But it doesn't matter which one you do first because it comes to the same amount. But if you do the discount first you have an approximation on how much you're paying.*

Danelle, Laura, Alex, and Kiet also showed their calculations and wrote: *It doesn't matter because it comes out the same. A certain number minus the discount plus the tax equals the same as if you minus the tax then plus the discount.*

Some responses, however, were incorrect, incomplete, or based on erroneous thinking. Bryan, Brian, Joe, and Peter didn't answer the question. They wrote: *First our group will put the sales tax on to the price. The reason we would do this is so we can see how much sales tax there would be and to see how much money we would save with the 20% discount. We would really save 5% off the price because the 20% discount subtracted by the 15% sales tax is 5%.*

Sunhee, Stephanie, Steven, and Elena wrote: *We would calculate the tax first because you have to know the total price including the tax to figure out the 20% discount. Also because if you calculate the discount first, you might end up paying more than you expect. For example, if you have the discount before the tax you end up paying more because you don't get 20% off the total, you get 20% without the tax.*

Paul, Diane, and Joey arrived at the correct conclusion but didn't explain why. *Any way because you get the same answer but doing the discount is easier because you find 20% of the amount of the purchase then you subtract it then you times it by .15 and then you add it to your total and you got the answer.*

I had to face the issue of assigning grades for their work. I haven't found any help or guidance for how to best evaluate a quiz such as this one. Maybe the reason we give "fill in the blanks" tests is because they're easier to grade. But they don't give insights into how students think. Of the 20 papers from three classes, I gave 10 of them a grade of A, and I gave B, C, or D to the others. I based my evaluations on the correctness of their answers and the completeness and clarity of their explanations. It would be good to discuss papers such as these with colleagues so we could explore together how to deal more effectively with the responsibility of giving grades.

An Individual Quiz—Using Percents to Analyze Statistics

I also wrote a quiz for the students to take individually. On the day of the quiz, I had the students indicate on a class graph how many pets they had. I didn't process the graph with them but asked them to use the information on it for one question on the quiz.

For the quiz, I drew a graph as shown that gave results for an imaginary class. I wrote three questions. It's important to note that this assessment didn't isolate percents but embedded their use in a statistical context. The emphasis was on having students use percents to reason through a situation. Also, the students were asked to present their reasoning rather than merely providing answers.

Name _____

PERCENTS—An Individual Quiz

How Many Pets Do You Have?

0	1	2	3	4	5	6	7	8 or more
x	x	x	x	x		x		
x	x	x	x	x				
x	x	x		x				
x	x	x						
	x	x						
	x	x						
	x							

1. About what percent of the students on the graph above have fewer than three pets? Explain how you figured your answer, even if you used a calculator.

2. Explain why you think this statement is true or false: About 25 percent of the class on the graph above has two pets.

3. Compare the graph above with our class graph. Describe how the information is *alike* and *different*.

There was a spread in the results. For example, when comparing the class graph to the graph on the quiz, Kim focused on the information provided in each and described several ways the graphs were alike and different. She wrote: *Their graph is like ours because they're asking the same question, "How many pets do you have?." Also, they both have zero in columns 5 and 7. And they both have 1 under 6. The median is different. Our graph is 1 and the other graph is 2. The mean is also different. Ours is 2.3 and theirs is 1.8. Our range is also different. Ours is 0 10 and theirs is 0–6. Our mode is different. Our most is 0 and their most is 1.*

Ray, however, did not analyze the information on either. He wrote: *Our class graph is like this one because the columns are the same and the way it is organized is the same. The way our class graph is different is that we don't use Xs. We use magnets. That's it.*

The students' responses indicated who were strong in their understanding and who needed more experience, continued guidance, and time. I've typically had this spread in my classes. But from lessons and assessments such as these, I not only learned which students needed more help, but I also learned a great deal about their thinking processes and about their specific misunderstandings and confusions.

Final Thoughts

Most traditional textbook programs put the instructional focus on teaching specific algorithms for each of three types of percent situations. Students learn procedures and are given problems to solve that call for applying the methods they've learned.

In contrast, the lessons suggested in this chapter presented problems to students that required they use percents in a variety of contextual situations. Few procedures for solving these problems were taught. Students were challenged to make sense of the situations, create methods that they thought were useful, explain why their methods were sensible, arrive at solutions, and justify the reasonableness of the solutions.

Making teaching decisions during the course of a unit raised complex issues for me. What direct teaching should I do? When is it a good idea to show students a particular method, and when will showing interfere with their learning? What should I do about those students who don't seem to figure out methods that make sense to them, who aren't learning to deal with percents effectively in situational contexts? Is it appropriate to give students practice? If so, what kind of practice?

The answers to questions such as these are the matter of the craft of teaching. I attempted to address these issues in the lessons in this chapter, not according to a checklist, but woven into the contexts of the classroom experiences. In the end, however, I know that individual professional judgments are at the heart of making appropriate decisions in these regards.

I also know that the next time I teach about percents, my experiences won't be the same. I'll have had the chance to tinker with these lessons. I'll have learned about new lessons to try. Different students will respond in different ways. What I try to keep in mind, however, is that just as I want students to become interested in math challenges that call for thinking, reasoning, and solving problems, I want to approach teaching with that same spirit.

REFERENCES

Bennett, Albert, Eugene Maier, and L. Ted Nelson. *Unit I: Seeing Mathematical Relationships*. Math and the Mind's Eye. Salem, Oreg.: The Math Learning Center, 1988.

Burns, Marilyn. *Mathematics for Middle School: A Series of Three Videotapes*. New Rochelle, N.Y.: Cuisenaire Company of America, 1989.

California State Department of Education. *Mathematics Model Curriculum Guide, Kindergarten Through Grade Eight*. Sacramento, Calif.: California State Department of Education, 1987.

Cowley, Geoffrey, and Karen Springen. "Faces from the Future." *Newsweek*, 13 February 1989.

Duckworth, Eleanor. *The Having of Wonderful Ideas*. New York, N.Y.: Teachers College Press, 1987.

"Harper's Index," *Harper's Magazine*, October 1989.

Mason, John, Leone Burton, and Kaye Stacey. *Thinking Mathematically*. Menlo Park, Calif.: Addison-Wesley, 1982.

Mathematical Sciences Education Board. *Reshaping School Mathematics: A Philosophy and Framework for Curriculum*. Washington, D.C.: National Academy Press, 1990.

National Council of Teachers of Mathematics. *Curriculum and Evaluation Standards for School Mathematics*. Reston, Va.: National Council of Teachers of Mathematics, 1989.

Phillips, Elizabeth, Glenda Lappan, Mary Jean Winter, and William Fitzgerald. *Probability*. Middle Grades Mathematics Project. Menlo Park, Calif.: Addison-Wesley,1986.

Scaaf, Oscar, Richard Brannan, Maryann Debrick, Judith Johnson, Glenda Kimerling, Scott McFadden, Jill McKenney, and Mary Ann Todd. *Problem Solving in Mathematics, Grade 7*, Lane County Mathematics Project. Palo Alto, Calif.: Dale Seymour, 1983.

Shroyer, Janet, and William Fitzgerald. *Mouse and Elephant: Measuring Growth*. Middle Grades Mathematics Project. Menlo Park, Calif.: Addison-Wesley, 1986.

Szetela, Walter, and Douglas T. Owens. "Finding the Area of a Circle: Use a Cake Pan and Leave Out the Pi," *Arithmetic Teacher*, May 1986, 12–18.

Tarshis, Barry. *The "Average American" Book*. New York, N.Y.: New American Library, 1979.

Zinsser, William. *Writing to Learn*. New York, N.Y.: Harper & Row, 1988.

INDEX

benefit to students, 85, 122, 123
cooperative, 109
organizing within, 42, 118, 138
teacher's role in, 51
value of, 72, 150
working in, 53, 64
Guidelines for using statistical information, 160

Homework, 19, 32, 51, 52, 53, 57, 62, 77, 97, 104,
    132, 135, 150, 158, 168, 170, 177
processing, 77

Learning
    and free exploration, 8, 9, 108
    by rote, 2, 90, 154, 156, 163, 182
    through expression of ideas, 1, 86, 150
    connecting new and old experiences, 24
    student participation, 33, 150
    through construction and understanding, 90
    through investigation, 1, 86, 150, 155

Materials,
    and need to explore, 95
    Color Tiles, 7, 8, 48, 65, 70
    Cuisenaire Rods, 81
    hinged mirrors, 92, 95, 97, 98
    interlocking cubes, 58
    Pattern Blocks, 91–94, 98, 99, 104, 108
    protractor, 91, 92, 105
Mean, fair and unfair, 65
Measurement, 2, 58, 137
    of angles, 95
    of area, 109
Multiplication, 30, 152, 153, 155, 163

Number, as concept, 2

Octagon, and circle, 120, 124

Patterns, 62, 75
    growth of squares, 56
    growth, 41, 43
    repeating, 42
Percent, 3, 137–182
Prediction
    and cubes, 59
    and patterns, 42, 43
    from a sample, 71, 78
Probability, 65–79
    and fractions, 65, 73
    and sampling, 73
Problem solving
    with a protractor, 108
    with concrete materials, 58–59, 62, 77
    with Cuisenaire Rods, 82–83
    figuring tips, 156–163
    price of pizza, 135–136

school population, 152
The Hamburger Problem, 173
The School Bus Problem, 150–160
The Xerox Problem, 175–176
Protractor, 91, 92, 105

Quadrilaterals, 104

Randomness, 65, 73
Ratio and proportion, 81–90
Reasoning, and need to explain answers, 71, 87
Reasoning, logical, 7, 152, 154
Rectangles, 58
Riddles, 7–22

Sampling experiment, 65
    and probability, 73
    statistical, 78
Shape
    irregular, 136, 146
    polygon, irregular, 111
    spatial model, 146
    "curvy" parallelogram, 131
    hexagon, 104, 111
    parallelogram, 111
    trapezoid, 111
    triangles, 103, 104, 111
Square units, 111
Square
    circumscribed, 114, 115
    finding area of, 114
    inscribed, 114, 115, 130
Statistics, 137
Summarizing, 22, 40, 64, 79, 136, 182

Triangles, equilateral, 102
Triangles, vertex of, 102

Videotape, 7, 23, 81, 92, 138

Word problem, 175
Working together, 16–17, 31, 36, 37
Working with partner, 31, 36
Worksheet, 31, 147
    finding area of a circle, 112–113
    Sense or Nonsense, 138–139, 144
    What Percent Is Shaded?, 147–149
Writing
    student's samples of, 18, 20, 21, 26, 27, 28, 29,
        31, 35, 38, 39, 54, 55, 57, 59, 61, 62, 63, 64,
        70, 78, 84, 88, 96, 100, 103, 106, 107, 124–
        125, 126–127, 133, 134, 140–143, 152, 163,
        164, 168, 169, 171, 172, 177, 181
    student's value of, 19, 27, 62, 69, 133, 145, 170
    student's, importance of, 118–119, 122
Written instructions, value of, 14